Give Me a Minute, Sweety

By

Alison Hodson-Robinson

Published by Noble Legacy Publishing

www.noblelegacypublishing.co.uk

ISBN: 978-1-911761-25-9

Dedication

This book is dedicated to all those who endure and suffer with mental health issues, whether they be solely psychiatric illnesses or disorders, or mystical and psychic experiences that have been misunderstood or overlooked. The line between the two is often very thin.

I offer you love, peace, comfort, and strength. May your voices be heard, your wisdom recognized, and your knowledge known

Introduction

Mental illness is often a topic discussed in hushed tones, surrounded by stigma, or reduced to clinical terms. Yet behind these labels are real lives, families held together, and silent battles fought every day.

Give Me a Minute, Sweety is not a story of defeat but a story of survival, awakening, and love. Through psychosis, psychiatric care, spiritual awakening, and the trials of motherhood, Alison Hodson Robinson reveals her raw and unfiltered truth.

This book invites you to walk alongside her journey, experiencing the pain, chaos, healing, and, ultimately, the transformation that unfolds when one refuses to give up.

Table of Contents

About the Author

Alison Hodson Robinson is a mother, writer, and mental health survivor who has lived through the extremes of psychosis, the rigidity of psychiatric systems, and the liberating path of spiritual awakening. Drawing from her own lived experience, she shares her story to give hope to those who may feel trapped in darkness and to challenge the stigma that surrounds mental illness.

Alison now devotes her life to healing, truth-telling, and inspiring others to see that even in the deepest struggle, there is always a way forward.

In The Beginning

I was born at approximately 10:30 PM on August 30th, 1971, the year of decimalisation in Great Britain. My parents had been trying for four years without contraception, unaware that they could actually conceive, according to my mother. She often shared the story of my unexpected arrival, and I always felt a little special, knowing how many eggs did not fertilise before I came along. That fact became a source of strength and purpose for me, especially during tough times. I'm 45 now and still do not quite know how I've made it this far, but I'm here to tell my story.

Carol and Frank, my parents, married young; she was 18, and he was a few years older. I came along when Carol was just 20, a big surprise due to her lack of knowledge about conception. She would later recount how she discovered she was pregnant amidst fits of laughter. She had walked up the hill to a telephone box to call the doctor after not feeling well, only to be congratulated on her pregnancy. "Oh no, that's not me," she replied, thinking the receptionist had mixed her up with someone else. The back-and-forth continued until my mother finally accepted, in shock, that she was indeed pregnant.

When she returned home to share the news with Frank, she was just as stunned. "You'll never believe it, Frank, I'm pregnant!" Looking back, it's hard to believe how uninformed they were about conception, especially with the availability of the contraceptive pill, but that was their reality at the time. As I grew older, I loved hearing the story of how I came into the world.

My childhood was not particularly happy. I became an anxious child, and I suspect I've always been highly sensitive. Carol, too, was emotionally scarred from her childhood of neglect and was highly strung, a trait I inherited and spent years trying to overcome. Frank, on the other hand, was a simple soul—pleasant, comical, and someone I adored. His eventual absence from my life was heartbreaking, likely a contributing factor to my struggles with unhealthy relationships and low self-esteem. I had no siblings or male peers, and attended an all-girls high school. Men were a mystery to me, and I found them intimidating. I learned the hard way.

Their marriage lasted only a few years after my birth, with frequent arguments about parenting styles. Carol was harsh, strict, and shrill due to her upbringing, while Frank was the opposite. He came from a rough-and-ready family in Leigh, while Carol was from a more affluent working-class family. My nan, Betty, must have had a heart attack when Carol brought Frank home. Carol was eager to marry and escape Betty's home, where she had never wanted to be a mother. Betty had been forced into a marriage she did not want due to her father's pressure, and her bitterness grew over time.

When Carol suffered a brain haemorrhage, Betty had to take me in temporarily while Carol recovered. However, Carol never fully recovered and was never able to parent as she had hoped. Looking back, I realised that perhaps it was for the best, given Carol's nature and my anxiety. The memories of my mother's angry outbursts, especially when I did not meet her unrealistic expectations, still send chills down my spine. My dad, trying to reason with her, would remind her I was just a child. Her perfectionist expectations of me would leave lasting scars, ones that influenced my own parenting style when I became a mother.

Carol was lovely, but as I've mentioned, deeply affected by her childhood. When she was younger, my nan would punish her for wetting the bed by making her stand naked all night. I do not think Betty was cruel, but rather, that was the extent of what she knew how to do. This harsh treatment left lasting emotional scars on Carol, who would spend much of her adult life healing from her past, as well as the aftereffects of the brain haemorrhage that left her disabled in many ways—though none were visible. Both my nan and Carol were wonderful women, shaped by their harsh upbringings and environments.

Alice, the matriarch of a family of ten, had the kindest heart. I met her a few times as a child, and I still remember her gentle, loving presence. She radiated warmth and laughter, though I'm sure being one of ten children made it difficult to feel that love consistently. Her husband, my grandfather, was a strict man whom I never met, and I have no second-hand stories about him from either of the women in my life. Perhaps he passed away young.

I do not recall the moment or the exact day my parents

split, only the aftermath—when my dad, presumably, would have taken me out for the day. He moved back to Leigh to live with his mother, and I guess he would come, as arranged, to pick me up. On one such occasion, when I was about four years old, he was standing in the hall ready to leave. I begged him to stay the night. Mum and dad discussed it between themselves, and the conclusion was, "Not tonight, Alison. Perhaps next time." The emotional pain of my dad leaving again was overwhelming. I do not remember much of their time together before the split, just arguments and a few small, pleasant memories. I remember waiting for dad to come home from work, where he would be given his tea on a blue Pyrex plate. I would hang around the table like a hungry puppy, hoping for one of his delicious homemade chips, which seemed to taste like heaven.

It was on one of these Saturdays, when dad was due to pick me up, that Mum's brain haemorrhage struck. That morning, I found her on the bathroom floor on her hands and knees, blood and faces scattered around, with an overwhelming sense that something was terribly wrong. Still conscious, Carol told me to go downstairs and wait for daddy. I remember thinking that if I knew how to ring an ambulance or call Nanny, I would, but I could not even reach the phone, let alone use it. Eventually, Mum made it downstairs and sat with me on the sofa. I asked if she was okay, to which she honestly replied, "No." We sat there, suspended in time, waiting for my father to arrive. As I write these words, it becomes clear that my anxiety in adult life may stem from this unconscious experience—the waiting and the trauma, which I now realise goes further back than I had thought. I'm certain the trauma within me has multiple origins and is deeply ingrained in my being. Healing will take time, but I'd say I'm halfway there, if not further, focusing on positive thinking wherever possible.

I do not know how long we sat there, but eventually, Dad showed up, and my life would never be the same. Mum was rushed to the hospital, and I was taken to my grandparents' house, where I would stay until I left home at 17. Mum survived but was never the same again; her brain function suffered, and her ability to function as a human being was impaired. She became more like an estranged older sister than my ill mother as my life unfolded with my grandparents. My Nan once told me that social services had planned to take me into care if Mum had not become ill, due to her not sending me to school, among other things. Mum's behaviour was described as "strange" in terms of parenting, but I'm unsure in what way. Over the years, I heard my Nan's stories about people I knew, and I learned her interpretations of reality were often questionable, so I took everything with a pinch of salt. Despite this, I did have a social worker due to the situation, and my grandparents became my legal guardians. At the age of 8, my surname was changed to theirs for simplification, particularly when traveling abroad.

Grandad was a lovely, gentle man—fairly quiet, clever, and wise. He was a television engineer who once helped build a set from plans when they first came out, according to Betty. He once gave me a bottle of mercury to play with. It was the most fascinating thing I had ever seen—liquid metal. It turns out, though, it's highly poisonous. As a clever and wise man, I can only assume he knew what he was doing and was not trying to harm me. It was a bit of a disappointment when I found out Dougie was not my real grandad but my Nan's second husband. Still, this did not change how much I loved him, and his calming presence was greatly missed after his passing when I was 15. I only lasted two years with my Nan before leaving home, clueless and totally unprepared for the outside world, after a fairly sheltered and strict upbringing.

When I was a child, my childhood was okay. But as I grew into a young adult and ventured into the world, it became obvious how ill-equipped I was socially and emotionally. I came to realise how much better things could have been had I been better nourished. Yes, I had food, clothing, toys, and holidays, but the demonstrative love and emotional nourishment I needed were sadly missing. My dad would visit me at first every week, then it became every month, then just on birthdays, Easter, and Christmas. I can imagine Betty made it very difficult for Frank to maintain a relationship with me, often negating him for his apathy. I never heard my dad's side of the story. He remarried when I was about 8, and I would go and stay with them, but I was shockingly anxious. So much so that, instead of going to the toilet at night, I would urinate on the bedroom carpet for fear "of being seen." Therapy at 29 would eventually uncover the reason behind this. I was terrified of bumping into my dad or his wife in the hall, even though I had no reason to fear them. They were strangers to me, and I was a nervous wreck.

I was lucky enough to travel abroad twice a year and holiday in Britain at least once. I had a much better standard of living than I would have had if my parents had stayed together or if I had lived with my mother. Overall, things were fairly normal despite the circumstances, except when my Nan could not cope with something I had done, usually not being perfect, and then resentment would fly out of her. She would say how she wished she'd never taken me in, that my mum did not want me, my dad did not want me—blah, blah, blah. She would often threaten to have social services take me away. As a parent now, I can understand this threat, but to a young Alison, already dreadfully anxious and insecure, it only added to my feelings of insecurity.

It was not the best way to Mold a well-rounded individual, but I forgave her long ago. It's true that she did her best. Psychotherapy at 29 helped me a lot with my childhood issues, including the realisation that I was angry with my father. I had always put him on a pedestal, mainly because at least he'd never made me cry.

There was a lot of drama in my childhood, it seemed, with my mum and her strange behaviour, including a couple of suicide attempts, and her being at my Nan's house after one of three operations on her brain. I remember her, complete with a shaved head and looking zombie-like from medication, asking, "Who are you? Where's my mum?" At the time, I was rather blasé about it; it seemed normal. It was not until years later, when I analysed the situation, that it caused me emotional upset. It was grief, in a way, for the loss of a "normal" life.

In therapy at 29, I had a major breakthrough during session 15 of 20: the loss of a normal childhood with my parents was the root cause of much unconscious pain and sorrow. Even now, I often feel as though I'm missing something in my current reality, and it's been suggested that this could relate to that time. I feel that I've come to terms with my childhood and no longer see myself as a victim of it, but it took a lot of work to heal and gain a non-victim mentality. What a sensitive soul I was—and still am, for sure.

My First Brush with Psychosis

At 22, I was single and working as a waitress in a hotel in Blackpool. I was carefree, socialising with my friends, many of whom were gay and part of the gay scene. This new world offered an exciting escape, and I started dabbling in recreational drugs. Though I had given up drug use during my late teens, a bad experience with acid at 17 made me cautious. My relationship with Kevin, who was very anti-drugs, also played a role in my decision to stop. That experience at 17 had been terrifying — I'd taken the drug with people who did not have my best interests at heart, and when things went wrong, they laughed at me instead of supporting me back to calmness. It was a hard lesson, but a valuable one.

Going out on the gay scene in Blackpool was a liberating experience. Growing up in Blackpool, I'd often tell random guys I was a lesbian just to get them to stop bothering me while I was out with my friends. So, stepping into the gay scene was like a breath of fresh air. I could dance without the unwanted attention of drunken holidaymakers. The music and the atmosphere were incredible, and the occasional cat fights (without the handbags) did not dampen the fun. As I spent more time in the scene, I gained a unique perspective as an outsider within a subculture. It gave me insight into how heterosexuals were viewed by homosexuals, and although I dislike labelling people, it's necessary to understand the full picture.

I absolutely loved it. The best part was when my crowd

started heading to Manchester for the once-a-month gay night at the Hacienda, called "Flesh." Heaven on earth for someone like me, eager to break free from the constraints of childhood and immerse myself in an environment of wild abandon. My desire for danger, excitement, and rebellion reached new heights. Unfortunately, the mind-altering effects of amphetamines and ecstasy dulled my common sense. My life would never be the same again, leading to one of the most terrifying mental states I could imagine — a drug-induced paranoid psychosis. Although terrifying, it was also one of the most interesting experiences I've ever had, even though not for the faint of heart. To see your mind unravel in such a way — and somehow return — was truly eye-opening.

I spent nearly a year frequenting The Flamingo Nightclub in Blackpool, raving every Saturday night while on speed and poppers. Classy, right? But my path soon led to an invite to the Hacienda's "Flesh" night. As a teenager, I had been drawn to New Order and the idea of the Hacienda, so when I finally had the chance to go, I felt both excitement and fear.

The Hacienda was a huge, warehouse-like building, and initially, it was underwhelming, as it was relatively empty. But within half an hour, it came alive with some of the most unique individuals I'd ever encountered. It was like a surreal cabaret on acid. Some people were even baring it all, completely naked, flaunting their confidence. One woman, in only a pair of shorts and Doc Martens, had her breasts out, exuding an attitude of "this is me, deal with it." It was fabulous, and I loved every second of it. I was out of my depth, but I did not care. I felt like a kid in a candy store, my inner child rejoicing in the freedom.

It was the epitome of living in the moment. As I danced, the drugs made me feel completely at one with the music, lost in every beat. I had no care for the past, the future, or any worries. It was just the joy of music, dance, and the good vibrations of love and peace. For me, it was pure bliss, and I had the time of my life. But of course, it would not last.

After my first visit, I lived for Flesh night. I made it there a total of four times. But by the fourth visit, my mental state had taken a dramatic turn, and I was descending into a full-blown drug-induced paranoid psychosis. It was terrifying as I watched my mind slowly unravel. The drugs were not solely to blame; my personal life had also spiralled into chaos and insecurity. I had entered into a relationship of sorts with Simon, a more seasoned drug user who mixed in deeper circles. He was the only straight guy around, though I later learned that was a lie. He also lied about being a postman and living with two mates. I was naive and soon learned the harsh reality of the situation. He was an addict, disappearing every day to get his fix, although I never knew exactly what drugs he was using. To say the least, Simon was a shady character who enjoyed manipulating a naive mind like mine.

I made my bed and, like it or not, I had to lie in it.

For some reason, I really set myself up for punishment with

this guy. I do not think I've ever met anyone with such low compassion. My lack of self-esteem and self-love, combined with an unconscious awareness that I needed to wise up, kept me trapped. This guy was street smart, and I had plunged in at the deep end — the quickest way to learn. Not the best for my nerves, though. I've never truly hated anyone in my life, but this guy came close to evoking that emotion in me. Now, of course, I see him for what he was: a great teacher. As all beings are, in their own way. He taught me what not to be.

Simon's behaviour, like stealing from friends, would eventually leave me friendless and relying on him as my only "ally." As my mind slipped further into the abyss, my support network of familiar faces slowly vanished, and I was left to face my own demons — and his. In six months, we moved house six times to escape from people he had robbed. We'd move in the middle of the night to avoid detection, which only added to my sense of insecurity and loss of self. The stress and paranoia I experienced became intense, and I started showing symptoms similar to schizophrenia: auditory hallucinations, extreme paranoia. This was not the kind of paranoia you get from smoking hash — "they're talking about me." No, this was the full-blown horror of thinking that people could hear my thoughts and were discussing them. It was terrifying.

Coupled with the psychological abuse Simon subjected me to, and the immense stress of the situation, I had a complete breakdown. I knew it was a nervous breakdown, but I could not articulate what was happening to me. I had lost the ability to communicate. The art of conversation, of simply interacting with others, had completely left me. People became frightening. I could not even remember how long eye contact should be held for, and I would panic internally, afraid I was doing it wrong and that someone would challenge me. My nervous disposition reached a whole new level, something that could only be understood by someone who had been in a similar position. Reality itself became terrifying. I was totally alone in a world of confusion, where the TV became my guide. There was nothing sinister about it, thank God, just simple things like "go tell someone you've moved house" — even though the person would not really care about this information.

There was, however, some spiritual richness in the experience, as I got my first taste of oneness. At the time, I did not understand what it was. The darker side of amphetamines and their paranoia made it an unwelcome experience, one that did not make sense in my world. I'm not sure exactly when the psychosis started, but I know the descent began when my weekly Saturday night raves at the club turned into taking speed at someone's house on a Tuesday afternoon. And then again a day or so later. Eventually, I found myself temporarily homeless after a 3–4-week amphetamine binge, with all bridges burned. It was the worst nightmare for an insecure and naive young woman who relied on others for things she did not even know were missing.

I spent most of my time partying in people's houses, often

with strangers. This was a bad move for me. While I had been happy to dance all night in the clubs, here, I was restricted to sitting and talking. Without the energy of dancing, the speed accelerated my mind, my thoughts, and my worries. I became consumed by paranoia. People would ask, "Are you okay, Alison?" and I'd nod, but inside I knew I was far from okay. Yet I continued down this path of self-destruction, as if on a mission. It felt like walking a tightrope into the unknown, with no way to go back. I could only move forward.

Simon and I had parted ways, and I found myself with no friends to turn to. I ended up in a studio flat where I was not allowed to claim benefits and had lied about not having a job. My partying, once limited to weekends, had become a weekday habit, leading to the loss of my job. My usual trick of finding another job immediately stopped working due to a lack of confidence and my deteriorating mental health. I thought things would turn around, but they did not.

I had never claimed benefits before and was unfamiliar with the system. When rent day came and I had no money, the landlord, a former doorman who did not tolerate liars or non-payers, put my belongings outside with a demand to pay by midnight. That night, I managed to stay with a couple I knew through a friend, and they took pity on me for a single night.

Being homeless and spiralling into drug-induced psychosis was too much to bear. I felt completely alone in both mind and life. A complete nervous breakdown followed, but there was no one around to notice—just strangers. Even my mother could not see the depth of my struggles. She believed I was homeless because of drug use and allowed me to stay with her for a night, but her own concerns about her benefits situation meant she did not want my presence to complicate things for her. I understood her worries, but it still hurt. When I left her home the next day, I promised to "sort myself out" and go to the job centre for help. Deep down, I knew that would not be a solution for finding housing.

I turned to an old landlord who could not help but whose son I was friendly with. He let me stay for a couple of days. In my delusional state, I believed he would save me and put me back on the road to recovery. But of course, he could not. It was just another floor to sleep on.

With nowhere else to turn, I went to see a nun, Sister Audrey, whom I had known through a conversion course years earlier when I converted to Catholicism for a past partner. I felt she would be a safe person to turn to. By then, my psychosis had worsened, and I felt like I was being chased out of town as I walked to the convent. In my mind, I heard voices from behind the houses, saying, "There she goes, that mad girl. Where is she going now? The silly cow." I felt unloved, unwanted, and incredibly afraid.

Thankfully, Sister Audrey was home, and I felt safe. She took me into the parlour, where she went to get me some food. As I sat there, I thought I heard her voice through the tape player, discussing me with others in the building. Logically, I knew this was impossible, but I was too deep in my delusion to think clearly. She returned with a bowl of broth and bread, and I felt more grateful than I could express, even as I became absorbed in the role of the homeless person. She did not question me too much when I mentioned the drugs. She offered me help with finding shelter and asked if I wanted a church-based place. I opted out, as I was fearful of being "converted" like my mother.

Sister Audrey helped me find a bed at the Street life homeless shelter in Blackpool for three nights. I had never felt so blessed, as I had no idea how I would manage being on the streets. The shelter had strict hours—10 p.m. in and 9 a.m. out—and I wandered through the days without much memory of what I did. I did, however, see an ad for a bedsit at £32 per week, needing a £10 deposit, which felt impossible at the time. But, by chance, I bumped into an old friend who was kind enough to lend me the money until I got sorted. That moment felt like a blessing—both the loan and the trust placed in me by this old friend.

Eventually, I sorted out my benefits, and the landlord agreed to wait for everything to go through. In the meantime, I had applied for jobs, though my confidence was still low. I soon got a knock at the door from the manager of a hotel in Blackpool, offering me a waitressing position I'd applied for. Though I had no idea how I would manage with my mental state, I knew I needed the money and did not want to rely on the system. Luckily, the hotel employed people from all walks of life, and I fit right in. I spent most of my time at work, quietly battling my internal demons, convinced that something was deeply wrong with me and that I needed psychiatric help.

Around this time, Simon reappeared. I'd bumped into him at the job centre, and, feeling isolated, I reluctantly reconnected. I soon realised this was a mistake, but he did take me to the GP, who referred me for counselling. Though it helped a little, I could barely speak, and it was not deep enough to truly address my issues. Fortunately, I did not present as psychotic and avoided being medicated at that point. In hindsight, not being medicated meant it took much longer to recover, and I would be left with a personality shaped by the experience.

This struggle has been both a blessing and a curse, as it's etched into my personality in ways I'm still grappling with today.

I carried on with my life after recovering somewhat, a year later. I had been an anxious person before this, so you can imagine how much more complicated and intense the anxiety became after the psychosis. I would have been entitled to disability help, but I never knew. Now, knowing, I would describe myself as having acquired a neurodiverse condition. The nervousness and anxiety were always there, deeply ingrained in my psyche and my body. I always worked after this, but only in minimum-wage jobs. At 32, I decided I could do better and focused my mind on going to college. Just a year or two before, I had shuddered at the thought of going to college, saying it wasn't for me, but I did it. I completed the "Access to Higher Education" course for adults and loved studying subjects like psychology and sociology, while working full-time as well. I wasn't the best at academia, but I scraped by and earned a place at university. I was so proud of myself.

And So, Uni Life Began

So, there I was at unit, but it was not at all what I expected. The halls of residence and campus buildings were scattered around Preston, so it did not feel like there was much of a community spirit. And, obviously, being on a social work degree, the other students were not much fun. They were all deadly serious people, not your average students. During one of the first lectures, the tutor stated, "Do not do this course if you're wanting to help people" … That was when I realised, years later, that I'd lost my motivation and drive for the course and found alternative "learning" in the community, amongst what was deemed the "underclasses". When I started this course, the "underclass" was just a hypothesis of a subculture emerging in Britain, what I came to call the Jeremy Kyle generation – the kind of people who would be using the services of a social worker. Not to judge, but you know what I mean. By the time I finished uni three years later, the underclass was no longer a hypothesis, but a fully-fledged concept.

On the course, I made a connection with a girl near the end of the line, queuing up outside the classroom door. Her name was Kaleigh, and she was much younger than me. I'd expected all the students at uni to be fairly upper-class, even though I was not, but Kaleigh was from a disadvantaged background and had been drawn to the social work degree because her brother was currently in jail, and she wanted to help other youths in that field of care. Kaleigh and I soon became friends and hung around together outside of classes. In the following February, Kaleigh's brother was released from jail and was back in the family home. He started hanging around there again, despite being just 16 and living in a children's home, though he visited the family regularly. To cut a long story short, this was when I met Joe – an 18-year-old lad, on a tag, and quite clearly *not* boyfriend material, but there was something about him that I liked. He was laid-back, cool, and mellow, and nothing seemed to bother him.

The first time I met him, I was at Kaleigh's house when her brother and father were having a physical fight. I was shocked by the behaviour and felt really uncomfortable. The house was three stories high, and I was on the middle landing where the fight was going on. From the top floor, this handsome young lad emerged and floated past me, declaring, "I'm off, see you in a bit, lad," in a clear show of "I'm not sticking around for this drama, it's not on." I did not realise fully at the time what had happened, but after a spiritual awakening nearly ten years later, combined with the knowledge of energy and vibration, it became clear that I *recognised* his energy – and he felt like *HOME*. I've since been told by a medium using trance as a reading tool that Joe and I have lived many lifetimes together, which is something both of us had suspected and felt.

Anyway, it was not long after meeting that we became "drug buddies", and my focus on studying deteriorated. I started missing many lectures, with Kaleigh choosing instead to party. I had found my second youth, so to speak, and I was enjoying the break from adulting. I used to think that I had, yet again, "gone off the rails", but with hindsight, I realised that I'd simply lost interest in the course from the very first week when we were warned that we could not "help" people.

It was not long before Joe and I started becoming interested in each other in a more intimate way, and we became "friends with benefits." My intention was to keep things casual with this much younger lad, having always thought I would not be interested in a relationship with someone much younger, and that it would just be fun. Here I am today, 16 years later, engaged to be married to him with two children in tow. Who would have thought?

Joe had a very traumatic upbringing, having been adopted at 18 months old and subjected to physical, mental, and emotional abuse. I'm not going to delve into the full story as it's long and heartbreaking, and that's a story Joe wants to share in his own book. What I will say is that much damage was done to his spirit. When we met, he was coping by using drugs and alcohol. As he was 18, I thought it was just a phase, but it was not until years later that I realised he was an addict, using substances to numb his pain. Sixteen years later, he's a regular user of alcohol and weed, drinking and smoking once or twice a week. He calls it "regulated use," and he's trying to manage and work through his issues, which he's doing very well with. We have walked side by side through life, been great comfort to each other as two wounded children in adult bodies, and have survived. Now, we're hoping to thrive.

Back then, I had ended up disengaging from my course and getting into a lot of mischief with Joe. Eventually, we parted ways, and the tutors on the course contacted me, offering me another chance with two options: either restart the course or switch to a less intensive course called C.C.C. (Care, Community & Citizenship). After some thought, I chose the latter. With Joe and his friends out of the picture, I was able to focus better. I committed to the coursework, the course itself, and had a renewed plan and hope for a career in social care.

During this time, my mother passed away after a short illness, and I inherited her bungalow in a lovely area called Thornton, Cleveleys. A week after my mum's funeral, Joe called me and asked to meet. He apologised for how things had ended and the way they had fizzled out. I thought long and hard about it, considering that I was doing well at university, but I had a feeling that he was meant to be a part of my story, so I agreed to meet him. The rest, as they say, is history. I ended up selling my mum's house and buying a home for Joe and me in Preston. I continued my studies, giving them the full attention they deserved. About two years into our restarted relationship, we decided to try for a baby—something we'd discussed many times. I had my contraceptive implant removed, and within months, I was pregnant. I could not believe it. I had always thought I would never meet anyone I could trust enough to have a child with, and I had also believed that I would struggle to get pregnant if I ever tried. I had always thought I'd find the transition to motherhood difficult in the first month, and I would need a particularly special partner to understand and support me through that time. Despite Joe being so much younger than me, I knew he would be a great father and a supportive husband during this special but vulnerable time.

The pregnancy went smoothly for the first few months, and I thoroughly enjoyed the experience. However, by the fifth month, my anxiety levels began to rise, and I started to feel unwell. I became distressed and fearful about the future, feeling that everything was spiralling out of control. I borrowed a book from the university library on pregnancy and postnatal illnesses, aimed at mental health nurses and midwives. It focused on mental health during and after pregnancy and included a chapter on postnatal psychosis (puerperal psychosis), a much rarer condition far worse than postnatal depression. It also discussed antenatal depression, which I had never heard of before but found comforting. I continued with the pregnancy, worked as usual, and stayed on top of my degree. I found work, as a project worker/support worker in a supported living service for people with learning disabilities and/or mental health issues, to be a source of good support. It was a challenging yet rewarding job, which I loved, and I had some very supportive colleagues. In May of that year (2008), I graduated from university with a 2:2 Bachelor of Arts degree. I was just 1.5% off a 2:1, and considering I had not applied myself as much as I could have, I was pretty impressed with that. Due to my fluctuating mental health, I missed my graduation ceremony, but at the time, I was not too bothered. I knew I was not well enough to attend, and it would have caused me more stress, but now I often wish I had that photo in my gown.

By the time I was about seven and a half to eight months pregnant, I began experiencing bouts of extreme anxiety and panic attacks, which made me seek help. During one particular episode, I had stopped eating and was lying in the foetal position on my bed, alone, while Joe was at his sister's. I felt very scared. Suddenly, I smelled the distinct scent of baby milk in the room (there was none in the house), and the thought "feed your baby" popped into my mind. Without hesitation, I got up, went downstairs, and made a jam sandwich, which I ate.

On another occasion, while lying on my bed feeling anxious, I was overcome with a powerful thought: "I am evolving." It felt so strong that I was urged to write it down. I scribbled "I am Evolving" on the calendar, the only paper I could find. I was both shocked and comforted, feeling as though the words were coming from somewhere deep within rather than from my own mind. It left me bemused, wondering if I was losing my sanity.

Shortly after, I made an appointment with my GP and shared what had been happening, asking if I could try antidepressants to ease the symptoms. However, he explained that no GP would prescribe such medication to a pregnant woman and referred me to mental health services. Soon after, I had an assessment at a place called West Strand House and was given a follow-up appointment with a consultant psychiatrist. I explained my worsening mental health throughout the pregnancy and mentioned that I felt I would need some help after the birth. The psychiatrist prescribed me a mild dose of Prozac and assigned me to a community psychiatric nurse (C.P.N.), who I saw regularly throughout the rest of my pregnancy.

As my pregnancy progressed, I opted for a water birth at home, and everything was in place to support that decision, including a wonderful product called "Birth in a Box" that I had purchased online. Despite the intense anxiety attacks, I began using a hypnobirthing CD and practicing meditations, which helped me relax during my maternity leave while I awaited the birth. I was feeling ready, though there was still some trepidation. I had read extensively about childbirth during my pregnancy, even reading pregnancy magazines to prepare for labor. I was very organised—at one point, I even painted my kitchen at eight months pregnant and laughed at myself as I hoovered the landing ceiling one Saturday night. For a woman who had never been fond of cleaning, that was quite funny.

Joe struggled with the impending pregnancy. Although he wanted to start a family, he could not understand why I was moody at times, even though I would yell, "It's my hormones!" After the birth, he admitted he had kept telling himself that maybe the baby just would not come out—mainly because of fear and denial about the impending event. I had bought him a book about pregnancy and labor, written by a man, but he did not read it. My best friend Abbey had also offered to be a birthing partner, so I was not too worried about that. I wrote my birth plan in case I had to go to the hospital, packed my hospital bag, but did not think much more about it. My home birth midwife had reassured me that I would only go to the hospital in an emergency. I had also watched a DVD by Davina McCall on the joys of home birth, where she explained that mothers who give birth at home tend to experience less pain and feel more comfortable. I included an alternative birth plan for the hospital in my bag, though I forgot about it myself.

The midwives had been very busy and had simply hooked me up to a monitor, leaving me to progress with my two birth partners. I had not told Joe or Abbey about the imaginary pain dial I had "installed" in my head, and I had forgotten about it, so I never used it. By the time the midwives came in to stay, they had been popping in and out during the night, and I was in a terrible state. It did not occur to me to mention the near crash I had been involved in earlier. It did not matter anymore. What mattered was that I was in full-blown labor, and I was not coping. It was not serene and lovely—it was the worst pain I had ever imagined. To make matters worse, I had been inhaling Entonox like a madwoman, as instructed, but it did not sit well with me. It triggered my drug psychosis symptoms, and I became "psychic," which was freaking me out. I had no insight into what was happening, and I could not communicate properly because I was hyperventilating. The more I panicked, the more people told me to breathe in more Entonox, not realising it was actually making things worse. All the breathing techniques I had learned went out the window. I was just inhaling Entonox with every breath. At one point, they hooked me up to a tube providing an endless supply from the wall rather than a canister, and I kept inhaling it. Needless to say, I was beyond high. I started hearing the voice of my mom from beyond the grave and receiving messages about the midwives and doctors, like what kind of music they liked and other strange details.

Somehow, I managed to progress in labor to being dilated to nine and a half centimetres. The midwives were asking me to push, but every time I tried to push "down there... into my bottom," I could tell by their expressions and the things they said that nothing was happening. I had completely lost control and sensation in that area, and I was utterly exhausted. They told me the baby was in distress, and after much discussion, it was decided that I would need a C-section. A doctor came in to explain the procedure. I was terrified because I had always feared having an epidural, and I was certain I was going to die (apparently, this is a common fear during labor). I started telling Joe and Abbey how to divide my estate, convinced I was not going to make it.

I was wheeled away to prepare for the operation. By the time I arrived in the operating room, I felt so scared, and it felt as though the people around me could hear my thoughts. I was relieved when I saw Joe appear in scrubs beside me. I had been given pethidine in the last few hours, and with the epidural, I was floating—thankfully blissed out by the time Katey was delivered.

I could not believe it—we had a living, breathing baby. She was beautiful and had sandy-coloured hair, which reminded me of some of my nan's siblings. Then we realised the greenish colour of her poop meant she had passed meconium in the womb during labor, which was one of the reasons they needed to get her out quickly to prevent her from swallowing it. Joe and I were both in shock.

I remember being wheeled into the recovery room, feeling as if I were in space. My bed felt like it was tipping diagonally, as though I were floating in zero gravity. As I was taken back to the maternity ward, I looked at this precious bundle and sang "All Things Bright and Beautiful," feeling like I was in heaven.

Things get a little blurry after that, but I recall Katey being born at 2:50 PM. I had been awake all night, and after the intense trauma of the birth, I was in a high state of anxiety. The pethidine had worn off, and I was completely exhausted, starving, and paralysed from the waist down due to the epidural. Joe had to leave just half an hour after we arrived back in the maternity suite (another story for Joe's book, but suffice it to say, being left alone with my newborn baby in that state was the last thing I had expected). I had always dreamed of that first precious time together, just the three of us, but it was not meant to be.

I did not tell the maternity staff what had happened. First, I could not voice it, and second, I could see how busy they were. I kept asking for food, and they kept telling me someone would bring it to me. I had always read that women were given toast after labor, and I had imagined how lovely it would taste. But no one came with any food. I gave up. I could see how busy they were, and I did not want to be a bother.

Perhaps the staff had not realised that my partner had gone, and no one was looking after me. Yes, they were taking care of the baby—feeding and changing her, which was all I cared about. I looked forward to sleep, but it never came. Despite being completely exhausted, I was awake all night, and the hours quickly passed. I spent the night marvelling at this beautiful little creature in the crib next to me, who had entered my world. I hoped that I might get a few hours of rest the following day, especially if the nurses were still feeding and changing her.

They were also changing me, as I was numb from the waist down, and naturally, a lot was going on down there after birth. Eventually, someone brought me a sandwich—the last one left in the day room—and oh, how I enjoyed it. Had Joe been with me, he would have probably gotten me something to eat from the day room, and I might have fared better. I do not remember much about the next day, which was Monday, but after being awake since Saturday morning, labouring all day Saturday and through the night, then not sleeping on Sunday, I felt mentally drained. The only thing keeping me going, besides my strength and endurance, was looking at my beautiful baby, and I looked forward to going home and getting some sleep there.

I had heard other women on the ward say you could go home on day three after a C-section, and I remember my sister-in-law telling me that once I'd had a bowel movement and was healing well, I could definitely leave on day three. As Monday evening passed, I became fixated on my bowels, feeling like I needed to go, but I've always had a bit of toilet shyness. I began to feel paranoid about it, so I asked if there was a disabled toilet I could use. I cannot remember if I actually went to the toilet, but around 10 PM that Monday night, I finally gathered the courage to approach the nurses' desk and ask for something to help me sleep. The paranoia was getting worse, and I felt as though the nurses were assuming I was a benzo addict. They told me they could not give me anything and that only a doctor could prescribe something.

At this point, I should have asked to see a doctor, having not slept for nearly 60 hours, but the paranoia was getting worse, and my confidence was at an all-time low. I skulked back to my bed. Thankfully, I was still receiving regular pain medication due to my C-section, and I worked up the courage to ask for stronger meds, claiming that my pain was worse than it was. They gave me some stronger painkillers, which knocked me out nicely. I managed to sleep for five hours, but when I woke up, I was paralysed again. It took me about 30 minutes to get my body to move enough to pull the nurse's help cord behind me. The day before, I had walked around the ward and even been down to the shop, so I could not understand why I was paralysed again.

In the years that followed, I had a friend who had been a theatre nurse, and she explained how epidurals work. She told me that it was not possible to become paralysed again after the epidural wears off. I have a brief understanding of it, but I cannot quite find the right words. I think I was pushing myself so hard to appear okay and get discharged as quickly as possible that I overrode the effects of the epidural until my body eventually gave in and relapsed back into a paralysed state.

When the nurse came in, I expressed my shock at not being able to move, especially since I had been down to the shop just the day before. She began to help me get off the bed. After she left the room, I tried to continue bathing the baby and getting myself ready, but I was feeling truly awful. I was severely anxious, and I remember needing clean towels. When I popped my head out of the door to ask for some, a midwife told me not to walk around with the baby but to use the portable cot. I felt overwhelmed by this "telling off," even though the nurse had not been rude to me. I realised I was beginning to feel paranoid again.

By the time the next midwife came in, I had become very unstable. In hindsight, I now realise this was when the baby blues were hitting me. But with my last few days of illness and the birth trauma I had faced, I was completely overwhelmed and became manic. Actually, I was not just manic; I was hypermania. I thought the other mums were talking about me, and I even believed some of the nurses could hear my thoughts. My energy levels were sky-high, and I told one nurse, who was talking on the phone to a doctor about me, that I felt like I was "pilling" (a term used when you're on ecstasy). The usual rush of postnatal emotions had intensified in my fragile state.

I remember feeling like I was a psychotic mum, and I even thought they had to shut the ward down to new admissions because of me (I never found out if this was true or just a delusion). They managed to get in touch with Joe, and when he came to visit around 9 AM, he took one look at me and started crying. I was not surprised— I was rocking back and forth, stuttering, and had started to emulate the mannerisms of many of the disabled people I had cared for over the years. I guess I was doing this in an attempt to communicate with those around me, though it did not make sense to me until years later.

Eventually, someone from Psychiatry came to see me and presented me with three options. The only one I remember clearly was the option to voluntarily admit myself as an inpatient at the local psychiatric unit. However, I would not be able to have the baby with me. It seemed like the only feasible option at the time, but I was not in any position to make decisions, as I had become so ill so quickly and was no longer in touch with reality. So, yes, I chose to enter psychiatric care as a voluntary patient, and with that, my fate was sealed.

And Then Things Got a Whole Lot Worse (and a whole lot weirder)

I do not remember much about that day after the psychiatrist came and assessed me, but I know it was around 10:30 PM when they wheeled me off to the Avondale. It was the place everyone used to joke about, saying that if you did something funny or weird, you'd be sent there. And now, here I was. I can still remember being wheeled through the dark, silent back corridors in one of those backward-pulled chairs. Part of me felt apprehensive, of course, but another part of me was intrigued, even excited, to see how my life would unfold. If only I had known then what I know now. Maybe I would not have gone.

Once I was on the ward, it was peaceful—no one around except for the elderly night staff, a lady named Victoria, who was 83 years old. She was small, with beautiful black skin. She showed me around the kitchen, where I could help myself to food when it was open, and took me to my room. They had given me a private single room, given that I had just had a C-section. She also gave me a jug of juice to save me the trouble of walking to collect fluids since I was still unsteady on my feet. I got into bed, and before long, I found myself staring at the window. In the distance, I saw two black figures. One was about three feet tall, while the other seemed to go up and down in height from three feet to about nine feet, both dressed in black army fatigues. Then, a black dog appeared at my window. My mind labelled this as "Satan's gatekeeper." I was terrified, so much so that I went to the front desk to ask for medication, convinced I was hallucinating. I needed a sedative. They gave me an antipsychotic. I did not have the strength to question it. I took it and went to bed. I was still in a terrible state, but I slept well.

The next day, I managed to haul myself out of bed and walked down the corridor to refill my juice jug. Halfway there, I suddenly heard someone yelling, "What are YOU doing with that?" I realised they were yelling at me about the jug. I was too weak to explain that I had been given it due to my condition after the C-section. From there, my memories become patchy. What I do remember is the bullet points: I became hypermania. I was running around the ward, sometimes euphoric, dancing and raving like I did in my rave days, and at other times, screaming and yelling like a banshee about being separated from my baby. Oh my God, how painful that was. I roared like an animal, screaming, "I want my baby!" I had a little dog teddy that I had bought to give to her, to make it smell like me, so I could give it to my baby, who was without me. We had named the baby Lydia.

I spent a lot of time in the main corridor, screaming, crying, and doing yoga. I began to have mystical experiences—flashbacks to past lives where I believed I was a witch. I was doing spells that I had no idea how I knew. It was exciting but also terrifying. I had no insight into what was happening. What I did not understand then was that the gas and air, being a psychodynamic drug, had opened my third eye. While I was raving and hypermania, I could have burst my stitches. You're not even allowed to drive for 5–6 weeks after a C-section, yet there I was, a danger to myself. Still, I was begging for sedatives. I screamed for "blues," which is 10mg of Valium. They would only give me lorazepam. Years later, a healer friend of mine, Janet, told me I needed sleep therapy, like when someone's been in an accident and they're put to sleep. My brain was so traumatised that it needed rest. But I did not get this simple treatment. I needed at least a sedative injection to calm me down, but no, all I got were antipsychotics (Olanzapine) and the ineffective lorazepam.

I remember Joe coming to see me the next day. He asked, "Why have you put yourself in here?" I could not explain it, but he knew I was unwell. He was right, though – I would've been better off at home. But I was too scared, and I did not know my rights. No one had informed me of them, and I was afraid that if I tried to leave, they'd section me. I remember trying to get my suitcase, determined to leave one moment, then terrified of being sectioned the next. So, I stayed. For one week.

All kinds of strange things were happening, but I knew not to tell the staff. Every time I came out of my room, they were watching from behind a desk, writing down everything I did. Talk about paranoia. I was already severely paranoid, hearing voices, seeing visions. I had become fully psychic but could not decipher the messages. I was too unfamiliar with it, and I was incredibly unwell. I could not tell the difference between truth and delusion.

One day, I sat alone in the day lounge when the darkest, deepest voice began speaking from the switched-off TV. I froze in terror, shutting down my senses and ignoring it. I told no one. I kept flipping through the paper, only to see the evillest face on a woman in the photo – it had become 3D. I said nothing. I turned the page, and on the next, there was Simon Cowell's face. His face, too, had transformed into something pure evil. Even though I was disturbed by what I saw, I somehow understood it. At the time, *The X Factor* was at its peak, and I'd often joked that Simon was the real king of England, with all his money and power. On some level, I understood it, but I could not express it.

As I did my strange rituals—spell casting, dancing, etc.—it was as though I was watching myself. I kept thinking, "Please stop, Alison, they're writing this down." I could see by their expressions that they had no idea what was happening to me or why, and that terrified me. I had voluntarily placed myself in their care, but they did not know how to help me.

I only trusted those with green eyes, like mine. I had never felt more like a lunatic in an asylum. Even though I was there voluntarily, I felt incarcerated. I spent time in the stairwell, gazing out of the window, desperate to escape. It was as though I were climbing the walls.

That year, Liverpool was full of *superlambananas*—massive statues of banana-shaped cows placed around the city for the summer. I watched the news every day, and they talked about these statues on Granada Reports. If you found one and called in, you could win something. I kept repeating "superlambanababy" like a mantra. It became an inside joke for Joe and me.

The staff kept telling me, "Go and lie down on your bed, Alison." It was the most ridiculous advice for someone in a state of hypermania. I needed tranquillizers. My baby had been taken to the neonatal ward, and Joe, despite his own struggles with mental health and drug use, was deemed unfit to care for her. But honestly, he was fully capable.

Joe brought her in to visit me after a few days. I had named her "Katey" after a while, but during my pregnancy, I had a dream where her name was "Esme." Spirit placed her in my arms and said, "This is Esme." But Joe thought it was too strange, so the name was vetoed. In my heart, she'll always be Esme—it means "to be loved."

When Joe visited and brought her to me, I was too scared to hold her. The trembling inside me was overwhelming, but I did hold her. I was too unwell to be a mother at that point. I knew I needed rest and sedation.

After a few days, Joe's sister was granted temporary custody, but Joe moved into her house and took on all the night feeds. He did everything required. He was incredible. He brought me sanitary towels when I asked, without complaint. He hugged me, held me tightly, and assured me, "It'll be alright." I believed him.

I spent a week at the Avondale. It was a week I'd never forget. All of the wounds I thought I had healed, from childhood and from the speed-induced psychosis, resurfaced. I was raw, in so much emotional pain and distress. I felt as though I was being mentally handled by forces beyond my control. And yet, it was not just one person—it was Western medicine, British psychiatric care at its finest.

They told me a place had been found in a mother and baby unit in Wythenshawe, Manchester. I was now really terrified. I thought it would be like a house from a Channel 4 documentary, full of "rough" women, all deranged, with their babies. No one told me it was part of a hospital. The staff on the Avondale kept telling me I had to calm down if I wanted a place at the unit. How I managed to calm down, I have no idea. But I must have done because, one day, I went in a taxi with a staff member. I knew my precious Katey would be joining me there, brought by a social worker. Unfortunately, I was not in any fit state to look after a baby. However, in Western medicine, it's deemed crucial for mother and baby to bond in the first few days. I knew about attachment theory and how important physical contact is between newborns and mothers, and I did everything I could to develop that bond, despite being out of my mind. But I was not able to look after myself, never mind a week-old baby for the first time.

When I arrived at the unit, I was surprised, but relieved, to find it was part of the main hospital. I was met by the manager, who told me she would be responsible for settling me in. I felt a little safer. She showed me to my room, then left to do something else. I never saw her again that day. There was no settling in, as I would call it. I knew nothing. Katey was cared for in the general nursery room at night, to begin with. After a few days, I asked someone how to get out of there and go home. I was told, "You're not even doing the night feeds." But no one had told me I could. Wanting to go home as quickly as possible, I said, "I'll do the bloody nights then." This, however, turned out to be counterproductive to my recovery and well-being. By then, I was on Olanzapine, a very strong antipsychotic, and a sleeping tablet, but had to get up every few hours to feed Katey. Can you imagine the sludge of the chemical cosh I felt? I was like a total zombie, dragging myself up the corridor to feed and change Katey. The trouble was, as I used to be a night-time sleepover carer, I always slept with one ear open, so to speak, and until I got used to my own baby's cry, I was getting up at EVERY baby's cry, only to be told, "It's not yours, Alison, go back to bed." The system was not practical. A mother in that position needed a good night's sleep to aid recovery.

I remember one particular night at 4 am. I had fed Katey, and she had vomited. I was so tired I could not change her and put her back in her cot covered in sick, hoping she'd go back to sleep— logically knowing she would not, but I was fried, totally. God only knows what the nurses thought when they found her in the cot like that. At that point, I did not care.

I spent six long weeks in that place. It's funny, that's how long the antipsychotics take to produce their "full therapeutic" effect. Had I been medicated properly, with tranquilisers for trauma, I'd probably, well, no doubt, have recovered much quicker. But that was not to be. The award was mixed with all different women. I remember one woman was very small with a very cranky baby, and her eyes were popping out of her head. You could see she was extremely exhausted and sleep-deprived, but still, she was caring for her baby all the time. Why on earth no one said, "Go to bed, we will take care of him," I have no clue. She was desperately in need of sleep. I was so physically tense it hurt to hold Katey in the crook of my arm. Still, my motherhood experience was painful. It physically hurt to feed my baby, and they kept taking my blood too. Oh, my God, it knackered me. I was so tense I could not physically let go and relax, and they took it anyway. One morning, I felt all of my life force zap out of me, and I could barely lift my arm. They took Katey for the day to let me rest and kept checking on me. I knew it was the result of being so traumatised, but still, I could not explain. I had no voice. They said when I came round a bit, they had been really worried about me, medically.

In the mornings, I'd have a shower, and at night, a bath. It was awful. Getting in a bath, hoping for that hot water comfort, but it was not there because my body was too tense. They'd look after Katey while I was in it, and I'd dread going back to that reality where I was a mum. I felt useless, the worst mother in the world. I was numb. After the hypermania, I'd sunk into postnatal depression. No warmth, no lovely, adoring feelings for my baby like I'd expected. I was just going through the motions. I fed and changed her. I held her, but nothing. No feelings—just silent despair.

Every Monday, they'd have a review. What an awful

experience. They were always running late, not by ten minutes, but by three hours. I'd be sitting in the waiting room with my CPN in a heightened state of awareness, still overwhelmed with extreme anxiety, psychosis, and trauma, dreading the review. There were about five people in the room: two doctors, a pharmacist, and someone else. It's tragic, but I'd been there a week before I realised I was actually allowed out of the hospital premises between 9 am and 9 pm. Nobody told me. I thought you had to earn it. So, then Joe would travel on public transport to Manchester to collect me and Katey, and we'd go home.

I did not enjoy this experience. Travelling in the outside world with this fragile baby as a new mum would have been hard enough, but due to the state I was in, it was terrifying. You had to cross Piccadilly Gardens to get to one of the buses (it was three buses back to Preston). I was glad to leave the unit, though, and I'd spend the weekend at home with Joe and Katey before going back to what felt like prison. I remember one evening, one of the doctors was around, and I asked him how I could get out of there and when. He said they were worried about me because I was crying all the time. Oh my God, is it any wonder? I still could not explain what had happened to me, and the medication made it even harder. I said I was heartbroken because I was in hospital, etc.

"Mary" (Poem)

"No, Mary! We do not get in the bath with our clothes on!" they

screamed at her.

Mary did not reply. Not that I heard.

I do not think I heard her speak at all that week on the ward.

She would just appear behind me, about three feet away.

Just a presence, a protector.

Her skin was as dark as the night sky. Her soul as old as the hills.

She was beautiful.

She was my friend.

Mary.

Coming Home

The six weeks I spent in the hospital were the longest weeks of my life. It felt like being in prison, and I had no idea when my release date would come. At every weekly review, I'd desperately cling to the hope I'd be let out to go home, only to have my hopes dashed and be given leave for just a couple of days. I could barely speak, so God only knows the personal hell I was suffering. I would have fared much better, I believe, in the community as I already had mental health support in place, but I was not strong enough to request and facilitate this.

I do not remember the day I came home or even how I got there, but I do remember the awful, deep, dark postnatal depression that followed me. I'd been taken off the Prozac I had been on before the birth, as it was thought to have caused my hypermania. I knew, of course, that it was not the cause, but I could not voice this. I begged my CPN to have it reinstated, but only after suffering for months. I told her it was ruining my postnatal experience and my life, and pleaded for her to let me go back on it. Every day was hell. I could not bear to get up in the mornings. Joe and I shared the night feeds between us. The lethargy was intense, and I could not wait to shut my eyes between every feed. I could not wait to go back to bed at night. I do not remember much about the days—life seemed normal to others, but for me, it was far from normal. I remember Joe trying to keep my spirits up. We'd get a babysitter and go for a drink, but my social phobia, due to the remnants of the psychosis, was too much, and I hated being "out there" in reality. He booked me a hairdresser's appointment during this time for my birthday, but I had nits. I'd had them for a while after catching them off Katey when she got them at nursery. I was such a mess that I went to the appointment, hoping the hairdresser would not notice. I was totally in denial. Of course, she did notice but was very lovely and kind, and instructed me on how to get rid of them. I already knew this information, but the depression and my mental health stopped me from acting on it. I was haunted by that hairdresser for years, as her shop was one of the local ones near me, and I often saw her in passing. When I was better, years later, I wanted to explain, but I never found the courage.

I was under social services for a few months because of the illness and had a support worker who took me to places like the local baby club. It was an awful experience. I wanted to scream out to the other mums and staff about how much pain I was in and that my reality was skewed. Extreme paranoia accompanied me there, but my beautiful Katey thrived, of course. Katey was an amazing, heavenly baby. She never cried, except when her nappy needed changing or when she was ready for her bottle. She never cried for no reason. She was not even ill until about 18 months old when she caught a flu bug. We used to put her down every night at 7 pm, awake, and she would gurgle herself to sleep happily. She was amazing. I often jokingly "blame" her for being responsible for me having my younger daughter two years after her—she was so good, we wanted another one.

I was only under social services care for a few months, thank heavens, as that was awful. Having to go for reviews with her and other professionals felt like being a criminal. I never did clarify on paper that I had not said I was going to throw Katey on the floor in the maternity unit, but that I had felt I was going to accidentally drop her. It did not seem to matter. Nobody wanted to talk about the past, only the present.

One day during my maternity leave, when the social worker had withdrawn, I suddenly decided I was off to baby club with Katey. It was a sign of my spirit poking through. It was not still a pleasurable feeling, but I felt good for taking her. When Katey was about 8 months old, my nan got in touch to tell me she had terminal cancer. She and I had fallen out after my mum passed away. She broke down in tears of joy when I told her I'd had a baby, which surprised me as she had always said to me, "Do not have kids." I then used to visit her weekly, travelling by train from Preston to Blackpool every Wednesday, and we'd go out for lunch. She absolutely delighted in Katey.

One particular Wednesday, I'd gone to baby club with Katey before visiting my nan. During snack time, Katey had shoved an extra piece of cut-up melon into her mouth without me noticing. When I turned to look at her, I saw she was choking. She was blood red and could not breathe. Out of nowhere, I found super strength and whacked her as hard as I could on the back, luckily dislodging the melon straight away. The two pieces came flying out. Nobody had noticed, and I never said a word, but I shook inwardly for the rest of the day.

Eventually, my maternity leave ended, and I went back to work, but I was not right. After everything I'd been through, my anxiety levels were off the scale. I only lasted a few weeks before going off sick. I was still under mental health services and on Prozac and Olanzapine, but I came off the Olanzapine. I'd realised I'd missed it for a few days in a row and felt okay, so I stopped taking it. It was about 11 months after the birth, and I found out it's recommended to take antipsychotics for 12 months after a psychotic incident. I did not tell my CPN I'd come off it due to fear, but after a couple of weeks, I did. They'd given me a working diagnosis of bipolar in Wythenshawe, so because I knew something was still wrong, I said I'd try bipolar meds. My consultant gave me a choice of two: lithium or Depakote. I did not like the sound of lithium, and you had to have your salt levels monitored, so I opted for Depakote, an off-license epilepsy medicine. Like bloody horse pills, they were—huge things, but I was adept at swallowing pills by now. They did not really help, and looking back, I have barely any memory of this time. I do not know how the hell I was still functioning, but I was.

I'd gone back to work after using up all my annual leave being off sick, afraid to go on actual sick leave due to the low payments of sick pay. One weird side effect was the dreams I had. They were so vivid and always anxiety-based that I never felt well-rested, even after a full night's sleep, as it felt like I'd really lived them. Also, I could not get to work on time, no matter how hard I tried. I'd always been the sort of person who got to work ten minutes early, but for some reason, I was always ten minutes late on this medication. My driving licence had been restricted due to the postnatal psychosis. I was allowed to drive, but I was on a three-yearly review now.

During this time, I developed a severe and debilitating lower back pain problem. I was prescribed very strong co-codamol, but they did not help. When I'd take two, I'd feel super disorientated but not fit to drive. At one point, I was taking eight a day, but it took me months to realise they were not actually doing anything in terms of pain management, so I stopped taking them. I was also going into work with extreme back pain. When I was upright, walking, or active, it would start—maybe ten minutes after being upright, or five on bad days. It was a thick, dark, dense pain that felt like it was pulling me into the ground. I'd find places to sit during my shift to alleviate the pain, eventually having to mould my shifts around what I could and could not do. In hindsight, I would have gone off sick had I been in my right mind, but I feel the tablets made me go to work in agony, causing further injury to my body and well-being. I think I was also afraid to go off sick, knowing how little the sick pay was.

But one day, I got home from a shift after my usual standing and walking in intense pain, until I could not stand it any longer, then sitting on a chair, a fence—anything to temporarily relieve the pain for a few minutes before standing up and starting again. So, yeah, I got home this particular day, got into a hot bath to try and ease my poor back. Joe had come to sit and chat with me, like he often did when I was in the bath, and I just burst into tears and said I could not do it anymore. We both agreed I'd have to go off sick, and we'd just have to deal with it.

Now, usually, my knowledge would have had me ring tax credits to tell them I was off sick on a lower income, but even though I was off for four months, it never once occurred to me. Being on a lower income, they would have increased my tax credits, but I believe the tablets I was on, the Depakote, curbed my reasoning and logic. Another weird side effect. Later down the line, I would win a court case against the council for council tax benefit backdating, and I explained that I'd been off sick on a lower wage, but the tablets I'd been on had stopped me from acting on claiming this benefit, due to cognitive blockage.

Eventually, I had physiotherapy, but the exercises they gave me I never did, still due to lethargy and lack of motivation. However, luckily, they also offered me acupuncture. I had six sessions, and after about six weeks, my back pain eventually lifted. I had not been able to walk to my nearest bus stop without having to sit down in agony or carry a shopping bag any distance, and now I was miraculously pain-free. Do not get me wrong, the pain still appeared here and there, but I'd say it was about 95% healed, and my life got better.

It took, I'd say, about two years for me to feel somewhat "normal" again, but I still felt dramatically altered after the hell I'd been through. Even after the speed psychosis, I described the postnatal one as "pulling the rug out from under me." My anxiety levels were higher, and the trauma felt immense. I was still on Depakote. Then, out of what seemed to be nowhere, came this crazy thought... to have another baby. I reasoned that having two was not so much more work than one, practically, and Katey had been so easy to care for that it seemed like a good idea. I also felt robbed of my experience the first time around. Part of me wanted to do it again... ok, so NOW I should have been sectioned! I always joke now that it must be because I'm from Blackpool, a famous seaside town with fairground rides, etc. I wanted to ride that ride again—the thrills and spills of excitement and fear mixed together. Deep down, somewhere inside, I knew they'd have to take me off Depakote, as the damage to babies in the womb from this medication was huge, and you could not even think of getting pregnant while on it. An unconscious knowing that this was my way out.

Then Along Came Rubey

So, somewhere out of seemingly nowhere, I said to Joe, "How do you feel about having another baby?" and without hesitation, he simply said, "Yes, let's do it," and carried on about his business. Well, that was that then, and I told my CPN soon after. It was recommended by the consultant that I go back to Wythenshawe Hospital to see the perinatal psychiatrist there, which we did. I felt very nervous going back, almost guilty, as though what I was doing was wrong. My nan had said, "Now you have your baby (about Katey), leave it at that," and obviously, because of what had happened when Katey was born, there were concerns.

It was decided between me and the doctor that I would slowly reduce off the Depakote and go onto an antipsychotic medication called Quetiapine, which I would increase towards the end of the pregnancy. This whole process took some time—months—and then I had to get pregnant. Funnily enough, it did not take long, even though by then, I was 41. Just a couple of months. I knew instantly when I was pregnant. I'd gone to the chemist to buy one of those early detectors, and lo and behold, it was positive. I was elated, and Joe could not believe it.

This pregnancy, mentally, was easier, and they changed my shifts at work to suit my condition, but physically, it was tougher. At three years older, I was also three stone heavier, but still, it was problem-free. I told the maternity team that there was no way I'd be giving birth naturally and demanded a C-section, which, under the circumstances, I was granted. The date was booked for one week before her due date. I had agreed to increase the dose of Quetiapine from 400mg to 600mg five weeks before my due date, but once I was actually pregnant, I changed my mind as I did not want my baby on that dose. I did not want to be on that dose myself, never mind a tiny fetus. I did have a few wobbly moments, of course, terrified of what might happen, but I'd been assigned a mental health midwife and had been going to yoga during my pregnancy, and the tutor helped me enormously with preparation for the birth. By the time the operation date came, I was ready, calm, and happy.

It had been arranged that Joe would stay at the hospital with me for three nights, and that gave me a great sense of comfort. The C-section went without a hitch, and the anaesthetist could not believe how chilled I was. It turned out we both went to the same yoga teacher. When I arrived at the hospital, the nurse checking me in was very young, and I said to her, "Do you know about my history?" She said, "Yes, but you're going to behave this time, are not you?" Oh my God... I could not believe it, but I said nothing, as I had other things to focus on, like keeping calm. They did not come for me until 1:30 pm, even though I'd got there at 8 am, but I was chill as anything.

Rubey was born around 2:00 PM, weighing 7 lb 15 oz, and was beautiful. My sister-in-law brought Katey to visit later that day, and we had cake. By the second day, I noticed Rubey's little body shuddering a bit longer than normal for a newborn, like when they do that falling action. I knew it was withdrawal effects from the medication, and the doctors had no treatment, just to monitor her.

I developed the most agonising pain in my stomach and reported it to the staff. They explained it was something called afterpains and that during the operation, the surgeons had physically handled my insides, hence the burning sensation. My mind, being a naughty monkey, tried to make me feel like a drug addict for wanting pain relief. Thankfully, I overcame that, and I was put on Oramorph, a morphine-based drug. After a couple of doses, the pain subsided.

After the second night, Joe went home to freshen up, and I ventured out into the main corridor for the first time since being there. I went into the day room to get some breakfast and sat down, but soon panic set in as this was the same room and corridor I had been in with Katey. Flashbacks began. From the safety of my room, I had not felt this, but now, in the thick of it, I was overwhelmed. I went back to my room, put Rubey in the mobile crib, and pushed her up and down the corridor as far as I could, up to the locked doors. I started feeling claustrophobic again, as though I was "locked" up. My emotions raged with pain and despair, and I could feel all the pain of the other moms on the ward. I knew I had to get out.

I remembered that my sister-in-law had discharged herself after her C-section, and I knew I could do the same. Out of nowhere, my CPN (Community Psychiatric Nurse) and mental health nurse arrived, and they could tell I was not right. I was basically climbing the walls and desperate to go home. They called the doctor, a paediatrician, who asked me what to do if the baby was distressed. I picked Rubey up and showed them how I comforted her, and they were satisfied with that. The shudders of quetiapine withdrawal did not last long in Rubey, and soon, we were ready to go home.

Getting myself and the baby ready was intense, and my anxiety about going outside was super high, but I managed it. My wonderful sister-in-law came to pick me up, and then we were home. The first night home was lovely. A friend visited, and we had takeout. The next night, I remember being in the bath, not feeling so good mentally. Racing thoughts and confusion set in. I got out of the bath, got dressed, and suddenly felt my body moving involuntarily, with energy not feeling like my own, as though something else was driving me. I got Joe to go out and buy some Valium from a neighbour, and I took 30mg. It was not much to me, considering my past with recreational drugs, but it worked. It calmed me down, and the rushing energy stopped.

Rubey was not as easy to look after as Katey had been; she was clingier. She would not sleep in her cot at all. Every night, after trying to settle her, we had to bring her downstairs, and she would nod off happily in her Moses basket in the room with us. At bedtime for us, I had to co-sleep with her, which I found a little hard since its controversial due to suffocation risks, but I felt it was the right thing for Rubey. I would place her in the crook of my arm, on the outside of the mattress, so she would not get crushed between us.

During the day, she spent hours sitting on my knee happily, and I loved it. It felt like a second chance to be a mom, and Katey adored her. I remember how hard it was waking up in the night for feeds. Often, Katey would wake up for a drink or something, and I would be so short-tempered with her, due to the sedative and grizzly effects of the medication—something I always felt guilty for. The medication also caused me to develop an overactive thyroid, a horrible condition that made me feel very unwell at times. I went back to work straight away after my maternity leave, but I had to take a lot of time off, not feeling physically right.

I remember once walking to work from the bus stop, around the docklands at Preston, and I felt awful in a way I had never felt before. I once read a description online of how an overactive thyroid feels, and it said it's like being a petrol engine, but someone put diesel in you. That was exactly how I felt. I had to go home.

During this time, I felt I wanted to give back in some way and help others who had suffered mentally, so I joined a research project for Lancaster University focused on people with bipolar and anxiety disorders. This was a year-long study, which entailed being interviewed at home about my condition, etc. After the year had passed, I began to realise that I did not fit into the bipolar category of the study, as the questions just were not relevant to my history and experience. I asked my CPN to see if they could finally officially diagnose me or review it, as I did not feel it fit me.

I had still been under their care all this time, having weekly appointments with my CPN and seeing the consultant (psychiatrist) every six months. After some discussion at my next CPA, my consultant stated that, with hindsight, the diagnosis of bipolar disorder was incorrect, and that everything had been anxiety-related. Wow. By this point, I'd been on psychiatric meds for six years. I was miffed to say the least, and I set about reducing the medication slowly. Nobody, least of all me, could have predicted what was to happen next.

Coming Home to Self

I reduced the medication under supervision, ever so slowly, even getting down to the last tablet, but cutting it in half. It was not until the very last bit had gone out of my system that things began to change. Obviously, I expected some anxiety, as I had it most of my life, and that's how the mind tricks you, too. I started to feel strange—like psychosis—but not quite, because I fully understood that part of it. I had insight.

I'd recently joined Facebook, and somehow, other people on there were posting similar things to what I was intuitively feeling… that I was psychic and magical. During Katey's birth, there was a moment where I became psychic and was told that magic was real, and then, boom, my waters broke in synchronicity with that. I always remembered that, and on the psychiatric ward, so many mystical, unexplainable things happened. Now it all made sense, but my emotions were all over the place. Six years of emotions being stunted by strong medication, and now they were all coming out. I felt as though I'd gone back in time to the birth, and people around me could not understand why I was going back to that. I could not understand how Katey was now six years old and kept asking how Rubey had come. Total confusion. I knew something bad had happened to me that was not my fault, and I was mad as hell with the NHS and Western psychiatry for what felt like being oppressed for six years.

Due to all the mental confusion, it took me 18 months to gain clarity and perspective. I started to realise I was suffering from

PTSD.

In the beginning, I did not dare tell the mental health folks about the psychic part because I was terrified of being put back on their meds. The anxiety was horrific, but of course, it was not anxiety alone; it was PTSD, which is much, much worse. I had totally had it with mental health services and went to my GP instead, who put me on an antidepressant for the anxiety. Nobody, including me, realised I had PTSD; they all thought it was just anxiety. I remember coming out of the mental health building in a hell of a state, and all they had offered me was the option to go back on quetiapine, which, of course, I refused. Thank God I was strong enough to say no.

Unfortunately, the antidepressant from the GP was causing mania-like feelings because I was not depressed. Due to the psycho and spiritual input, I was receiving, I was in a good mood despite all this furore. I knew deep down in my soul that I was safe and that all this was a process I had to go through. I knew, somehow, that I was in a new way of being and understanding. Physically and mentally, I was destroyed, but spiritually, I was strong as hell. The only tablet I would take now was diazepam, and luckily, we had moved out of Preston to a semi-rural place called Stalmine, near Blackpool, my hometown. The doctor there was pretty cool and gave me diazepam to help me cope. I used it PRN (as and when) as I knew its addictive nature and did not want that.

I was still going to work but pretending I was okay, apart

from the awful anxiety. By now, I was fully psychic, feeling energy, and had been reduced somehow to the atom. I knew reality was an illusion, and the only way to describe what I was experiencing was that my part in the hologram was glitching. I could see myself when I looked down, but I was not solid anymore. In fact, I was porous. It was like being on LSD, I suppose, but this was natural. Of course, the gas and air, due to their nature, had opened my third eye, as it's called, but the antipsychotics stopped that. When they were removed, it carried on. During this time, I learned about Kundalini awakening, and I believe this is what happened to me on the psychiatric ward postnatally after Katey's birth. But this time, I was able to understand it, and the spirit world was helping me through signs, symbols, and synchronicities. It was totally overwhelming, and even though I understood it, with the state of my health and the PTSD going on, it was intense and so much pressure. Hiding all this from my colleagues, too, was more pressure. Apparently, the more intelligent you are, the easier it is to mask your "symptoms."

I'd started to identify more with the service users than with my colleagues, and all I could see was oppression everywhere, whilst at the same time feeling and understanding that I was loved. Actually, not just feeling it—I knew it. Everything seemed upside down and back to front, and I was so angry about it. I was angry about what had happened, even though I still did not understand what had happened. The PTSD, which felt like severe anxiety like I'd never known before, was present daily. It felt like that shocked feeling you get if you hear breaking glass in your home at night—massive shock in your chest and total fear. For three months, I carried on with life, going to work but having to cope with this condition at the same time, using every tool and technique to manage it, while also dealing with being psychic and feeling energy. The pressure on my brain was immense, and I had a brain ache every day. Yet, due to the understanding of my spiritual awakening, I knew I'd be okay eventually. Faith kept me strong.

I felt as old as my soul, though, and was on 240mg propranolol, a headache preventer, daily, but it did not stop the physical pressure on my brain. How I did not have a stroke, I'll never know. Eventually, I managed to bring that shock feeling down to a lesser intensity, but I was completely burned out, both physically and mentally, from doing so.

I knew I needed rest, so I rang my employers and stated I was mentally exhausted and needed an emergency week off. I could not explain why; I had no words left. Even talking had become so difficult. I had my week off, but obviously, it was not enough, as this had gone beyond normal exhaustion. I believe, now, that going to work like this actually caused a brain injury from the pressure. When I returned to work, I had to have an interview because of what I'd said, and then it all came spilling out, and they realised how poorly I was. I was suspended on grounds of mental health, and this was my nightmare come true: I'd been outed as what I felt to be a lunatic again. The brain pressure then travelled into my brainstem, and I accepted their decision, crying and stating to my boss that I was just trying to work my way through my own consciousness (the spiritual awakening had taught me about this), and she understood but stated, most compassionately, that my consciousness, at that point, was a little more complicated than normal.

I went for a coffee with Joe afterwards, and we agreed on how poorly I was. I got dropped off at A&E, with a mind to getting medication. Luckily, I saw an Asian doctor and was able to say I was just struggling with duality. He gave me a prescription for diazepam to last me the weekend until I could see my GP on Monday. I was glad he'd understood.

When I came out of the mental health building that day, feeling exasperated and poorer than ever, I sat in my car, looked up at the sky, and asked the universe for help. I did not know what to do or where to go. After a while, something told me to go to Penwortham, to a juice bar there that I often went to, so I did. I got myself some juice, then went to the cash machine. I cannot tell you how insanely anxious I was just to withdraw money. Feeling energy, I had a different view of money now, and connecting with money or anything to do with the system was terrifying. But I managed. I saw a sign in a shop window saying oriental and cranial sacral balancing. I was immediately intrigued and went in. Luckily, the lady was in between clients and was able to explain the procedures. I was amazed and booked an appointment for the next day.

I was so badly traumatised; this was the beginning of my real healing, using holistic/alternative therapies. This lady was amazing. She was qualified in both Western and Eastern medicine and other alternative treatments. She confirmed to me what I'd been feeling was true: not all people with mental health illnesses were actually poorly, but were just awakening to their true divine natures and accessing their psychic and magical abilities. For example, if you list the symptoms of psychosis and schizophrenia side by side with the gifts of the psychic, they are basically the same thing. It's when your mind and consciousness open up to the supernatural, which is real, and depending on various factors such as your understanding, wisdom, support, and knowledge, you can cope with it—or not. The nation's potential healers are being misunderstood and shut down with medication and locked up in some cases. A lot of this can happen at the event of trauma, so people are not always able to process or integrate it. This was me.

I was so badly traumatised by now that I was carrying around one of Rubey's toys that was like a television screen and played a tune. The only way I could feel safe was by keeping pressing the tune to come on and soothe me… crazy. And I had the most awful fear of being seen as crazy. But I also knew my own particular brand of crazy was fabulous, and I had to own it somehow.

There was so much going on… PTSD was undiagnosed and possibly complex, a spiritual awakening, powerfully psychic, and I was also self-actualising. That's when you reach a psychological state where you can see your full potential and the same in others… kind of like seeing souls, not people. Of course, I was being shown about energy, vibration, and frequency. One of the managers at work, who knew nothing of my mental health history, spotted it... the self-actualisation. Funny, isn't it, that she did not think I was "ill"?

During the six years I'd been on medication, I'd never been offered any clue as to what psychosis actually was, and I had so many unanswered questions. So, I read a lot about the mind, including books like *Who Am I and Where Do I Come From?* by the great spiritual guru Deepak Chopra. This taught me about consciousness, but I did not fully grasp it at the time. I also read another great book called *Buddha's Brain*, which taught me all about neuroplasticity—something that really came in useful during my recovery. The knowledge that the body can heal from anything.

So, when I came off the medication, it felt as though everything I'd read finally filtered through my brain and out through my eyes. Not only was I put in touch with infinite intelligence, but I knew I had become, and was, pure consciousness. I knew I was everything and nothing at the same time. I've often said that some people would pay a fortune for the experiences I've had and the knowledge and wisdom I've gained. Little old me from Blackpool. Who knew?! Well, "God" did, that's who, although I prefer the term Source Energy.

I learned from my healer, the internet, Facebook, etc., from others who'd been through, or were on, the same journey as me, that you're only given as much truth as you can handle, or it overloads the nervous system. Well, the guy in charge of my dose must have been drunk or something!! I learned that the veil (of illusion) did not just thin for me—the whole nine levels (I seem to think it was nine, if I remember correctly) were removed all at once. It was both exhilarating and terrifying at the same time. It was the undoing of all I'd ever known to be true.

The healer had a partner who was heavily involved in the spiritual world. She was something known as a star seed. I immediately knew when I heard this term that that was me. I Googled it, and my mind was blown. A star seed is a being whose soul originates from other dimensions, more evolved than Earth. Yes, basically an alien, and I knew this was my truth too, as I could recall having what's known as the star seed awakening alarm clock moment. It was one Sunday evening at home, alone with just me and Katey. Katey and Rubey were both in bed. I was bored and went on YouTube to look at aliens and angel stories and thought, "What on Earth am I doing?" I had no previous interest in either of these topics. That was the start of it. This was when I'd finally reduced the last tiny bit of medication, even cutting the pills in half, then quarters.

As time progressed, I became, as I said, more psychic, feeling energy, etc., and this partner of my healer knew immediately what I was experiencing. She said, "You're walking the worlds," and I thought, "I do not know what that means, but it sounds exactly like what I was going through." The only way to describe it is that the back part of your head feels the spirit world... the other dimension, physically there. She kept asking me if I could see spirits, which thankfully I could not, but I was aware of the afterlife, physically, at all times. I was aware of how all things are orchestrated from up above, yet we all have free will at the same time. A total paradox that now I'm back to "normal," I have no logical concept of. All I knew was that I had to trust the process, and to heal, I had to learn to love myself. I was starting at a place of not liking myself very much.

I knew through the PTSD that the week I spent on the ward caused me so much emotional damage, not just because of what happened, but because all my previous childhood and emotional scars were reopened. All the stuff I'd put to bed was laid bare again, and I knew I'd been medically neglected and mistreated. This whole time, after coming off meds, I could barely even manage a doctor's appointment. I had developed a medical person phobia and only sought alternative treatments, of which I had many.

I tried everything holistic and not a tablet, and I was obsessed with all things spiritual. "Spiritual window shopping," they call it. I went to psychic nights hoping to get some reassurance, and the people I'd connected with around the world, like me, were my main source of comfort, love, and reassurance. My back problem had returned, so it definitely confirmed to me it was related to the trauma of Katey's birth. I was having acupuncture again with my healer, but it was not helping. I think there was too much going on in my mental and emotional bodies for it to work. So eventually, I realised my healer was not able to help me anymore, and something inside me said, "You need a shaman."

Shaman In a Concrete Jungle

That was about nine and a half years ago. Now, I am the shaman. I was then, but I just did not know it consciously. Shamanism is the oldest spiritual practice on Earth. It's a way of using signs and symbology to interpret messages from the other side, to facilitate one's own healing, and to facilitate the healing capabilities of others. A being who has healed themselves by using holistic healing practices, including journeying to the other worlds. This is done with the use of a drum, and the drumbeat creates a gap in the psyche where you can journey into your own consciousness and come back with your own answers.

People often associate shamans with dark magic, but that's voodoo—a different thing. I'd heard of shamanism once or twice but did not know much. It's about as psychic as one can get. There's a story of a shaman who came to the UK and visited a friend in a psychiatric ward some years ago, and was appalled at what he saw and how we treated our mental health patients.

You see, what I've come to realise now is that the gifts of a psychic and the symptoms of psychosis and/or schizophrenia are practically the same thing. Often, a mental health crisis is actually the birth of a healer, but in the West, we just do not understand it. The shaman saw his friend and others in straitjackets and was appalled. I'm not saying all mental illness is this, but a lot of it is—and this I knew from my own experience. There were too many magical and mystical things that happened on the psychiatric ward when I'd been admitted after Katey's birth and the trauma involved in that, things that mental health services and Western psychiatry just could not explain.

So, the past two times I'd been in what we call here "psychosis," I had no insight. But during this third episode, I knew it was spiritual, not mental, and I felt safe in that knowledge. When I'd gone into the shop of the holistic healer I was seeing back then, her partner was there, and she was trained in Tibetan Wicca, no less, which, to me, was the epitome of cool, what with me being a Buddhist type before the spiritual awakening, and now remembering my witchy roots. She looked at me and simply stated, "You're walking the worlds." I had never in my life heard this expression, but it described exactly what I was experiencing.

The only way I could explain it now is that the back of my head was all connected to the other side. I could literally feel the movement across the veil, as it's called, and knew instinctively that that was the other side. I understood numbers, time, money, and the strangest thing of all was language and words. One time, I spoke to someone in the schoolyard, and time seemed to slow down, and I felt the weight of every letter in every word the other person was saying. I learned about spelling, how we have to carve our words like stone, etc. We are creator beings, and everything we say is so important, especially how we speak to ourselves.

I knew that I was loved, and that love was the answer to everything. Self-love was now the mission I was on, which was challenging when you barely like yourself. During the time I was still at work, I remember being on shift one day when, through my phone, came the photo of a little Asian boy, and I read the article attached. It turns out he was the victim of extreme childhood abuse and neglect. His mother, being an alcoholic with mental health illness to boot, had starved this poor little mite. When he died, she left him in the cot and carried on with her life, all the while his little body decomposing next to her bed. She was obviously deeply disturbed and in another world.

The poor lad had been starved so badly that he was dressed in a baby grow meant for a six-month-old, even though he was four years old. His name was Mohammed. I cried like a baby myself. I kept reading it and looking at his photo and crying for England. Child abuse stories always upset me, but this was something else. I could not stop looking at his little face, and I felt his suffering and pain. I will never forget his face. I can see it now, etched into my psyche forever. Thankfully, I do not remember hers.

I was very upset for days about this. Then, one Sunday evening, around that same time, I was looking, as I mentioned in the previous chapter, for angel and alien stories on YouTube, which was very out of character for me. I started to search for the youngest premature baby ever to survive. I was looking for inspiration. What I found was a short video entitled *"Our Last Goodbye."* This was the story of a baby called Finley, who had been "born sleeping" (the medical term for stillborn). The mother was in it with him, and it was the most heartbreaking thing I'd ever seen in my then 42 years of living. I won't go into the whole story, but the crux of it is this: he was a full-term, healthy baby, but mum needed a C-section, and basically, they did not get him out in time, and he died without ever having taken one breath.

The video I came across was of mum explaining, via written word, that the midwives had asked her what she wanted to do to say goodbye. She said she wanted to bathe him, change his bum, and dress him. She wanted to make memories. The video shows Finley's little body being bathed and dressed; it's not graphic and is shot from a distance. I realised that watching his little body not respond to mum's touch and actions was the most tragic of scenarios. Newborns are supposed to be alive, especially those that were otherwise healthy. The amount of emotional pain I felt from this story was intense. I could not understand why it was upsetting me so much—I mean, I had never lost a baby in this way.

I learned years later in counselling that this is known as trauma via proxy. I followed the links and found the mother's Facebook page. She had many beautiful photos done of her, dad, and Finley in sepia. I literally became obsessed with this story, and I could not stop crying about it. It was not morbid fascination, I knew that. I was crying at work, at home. I was absolutely devastated. There was one photo in particular where the mum had her face pressed up against Finley's head, and the pain in her face was so primal and raw. I kept looking and looking, and then one day, I saw what I was looking for. It was the most heartbreaking thing, but I realised that there is no boundary between a mother and child—not even death itself could affect this. This was unconditional love. Raw, brutal, primal. The beauty of death, life, and all it entails.

When my healer's partner had told me about star seeds, she said some come to learn about unconditional love. This, I knew, was my story. Finley's mum and I were Facebook friends, and she herself has become a pioneer in the world of baby loss, campaigning tirelessly for cold cots and the like. She hosts the nation's Butterfly Awards every year. She wrote a great book called *After Finley* and created her own charity called *Finley's Footsteps*.

What was really strange was that this story was five years old when I came across it. But it had, as I said to Finley's mum, caused a massive wave of light, and its trail was still glowing years later. His heavenly birthday was coming up, and his mum asked me if I wanted to be part of the marking of it. I was sitting in a café hundreds of miles away in Blackpool (she lived down south), and she said it had to be related to feet, in honour of the footsteps part of the charity in his name. I knew immediately what I was going to do, and it was to have the name "Finley" tattooed on my foot in Chinese, and that's what I did. His and his mum's beautiful story is emblazoned on my being forever. And I know that women reading this may be helped by this story.

I recently told Joe about poor little Mohamed. He knows the story of Finley because he lived it with me, but I'd never mentioned Mohamed until recently. During the retelling of the story, I realised that the spirit world showed me two mothers, both with babies who died but in very, very different circumstances. The worst mother and the best. I was being taught about unconditional love through Finley's story. I do not know what you'd call Mohamed's story. It was then that I learned I was an empath. When I heard this, I thought, *WTF?* I thought that was a fictional thing, like Deanna Troi from *Star Trek: Voyager*, but no… It's a thing, and it does not end there.

Part 1

The universe revealed itself to me on an energy level, and I came to understand that we originate from and are, in essence, love. Love itself is energy—a physical force. I vividly recall the profound sensation I experienced when I came across a picture of the galaxy on my phone. The image sucked me in, swirling around, and in that moment, I knew that what some people call "God" was this very energy. It was an incredible feeling; unlike anything I had ever experienced before. It surpassed even the euphoria of ecstasy.

They say that as you draw closer to Source, you begin to experience more synchronicities. For me, everything felt synchronised throughout the day, which completely blew my mind. It was overwhelming to process, yet I understood that the world itself was magical and was communicating with me. The only other times I had encountered such experiences were during moments of trauma, where I was deemed mentally ill. However, I knew this was not an illness—this was real. Thankfully, I found others like me on Facebook, scattered around the world, and I realised I was one of the long-prophesied Rainbow Warriors.

The Hopi Indians had predicted many years ago that, when the animals were nearly extinct and the trees were gone, a group of people would emerge from various backgrounds, creeds, colours, and nations. Together, they would heal the Earth. They also mentioned a "spider's web" around the Earth—today, we know this as the internet. I knew then that I was part of this group.

Admittedly, it was a lot to process, and there were times when I felt crazy, especially since I did not talk much about it, particularly to psychiatric doctors. Without the support I found on Facebook, I'm sure I would have lost my grip on reality.

At the same time, I was grappling with PTSD. I felt as though the universe was putting me through a shamanic initiation, and yes, it was painful. In places like Africa, the Amazon, or Siberia, where the original shamans come from, the local shamans have always undergone intense trauma, illness, or near-death experiences. These trials gave them their wisdom and healing abilities, and they also came to understand plant medicine. In Christianity, the Rainbow Warriors are referred to as the 144,000. This number is notliteral; rather, it refers to a specific type of human incarnated with a different DNA structure, capable of holding and transmitting higher frequencies of light, influencing the frequency of the Earth at this time. Eckhart Tolle explores this concept in his book *A New Earth*.

Now, as I write on February 9th, 2025, after many breaks in the writing of this book, I realize that the timeline of the new Earth is here, following the split in dimensions. As a star seed, I have lived many lives on different planets and dimensions, but in this current human life as Alison, I am experiencing my role as a shaman. I now understand that the gas and air administered during labor opened my third eye, which, at the time, I mistook for a "psychotic episode." This is why I now experience PTSD— because nobody noticed this shift, and I lost my insight at that moment.

Of course, I wondered: "Is this all in my head?" But deep down, I knew it was real. The people in my soul tribe from around the world confirmed and supported my experiences, and in turn, I was able to support many others. Everyone has the potential to be psychic because we are all born with a third eye. This concept was once elusive, but we now know it's connected to the pineal gland, a small body part that resembles a pine cone. I often feel it throb when meditating or shamanic journeying.

Can you imagine going to work with all this happening inside you? It's no surprise I ended up injuring myself. Since then, I have not worked and am registered as disabled. Do not even get me started on that word... "disabled"? Like I'm turned off? I do not think so. I vividly remember telling my boss during my last official meeting, when I was retiring, that I would not be walking away quietly into the night. I was not referring to my employers, but rather to the system—the matrix—and everything it represents.

Now, ten years later, here I am, having healed so much of the conditioning and PTSD. Over the last 12 months, I've regulated my nervous system with the help of one non-psychiatric drug. I know it's not just the drug; it's the tremendous amount of inner work I've done.

Part 2

The healing years were the hardest of my life. I was in that very magical state of consciousness for about two and a half to three years, but with the PTSD, brain injury, and being a parent, I had to ask Spirit to turn it off. I could not integrate it, as they say. I had asked before for them to tone it down, as advised by other spiritual people, but it still became too overwhelming. Having been lost, so to speak, for six years on psychiatric medications, during those few years, I became very anti-medication. I survived all the stress on Valium, which I had taken in the past and knew the side effects were minimal for me. I used it occasionally, as it does not work when taken constantly. But without a shamanic guide, the darkness began to take hold, and I found myself in a mess. Eventually, I had to relent and take antidepressants again, followed by antipsychotics after a few months. This led me into a wilderness of hopelessness, feeling like a failure for not being able to complete my mission.

I continued as best I could, but I started using alcohol and cannabis to cope. I had not smoked weed in 20 years due to paranoid psychosis, so it took a long time to handle it again, knowing there were medicinal benefits. I used it a few times a week. Over the next six years or so, I seemed to experience every mental health condition going, including, unbeknownst to me, menopause. I just put it all down to me being someone with mental health issues. My periods had stopped, but I had no other symptoms, so I kept waiting for the hot flushes that never came. If I had not been so isolated, experiencing this in the "wilderness," I might have sought help for the mental health issues associated with menopause. But I was anti-medication for obvious reasons. I'm glad I did it "bareback," so to speak, because I would have struggled greatly with whether to use HRT or not, given my thoughts on Western medicine.

During this time, the PTSD was very tough, and I came across the concept of the "freeze" and "flop" symptoms. Every time one of my children said or shouted, "Muuuuum," I would freeze, not understanding why—hence the title of this book, *Give Me a Minute, Sweetie.* It was not until I met someone who told me about this symptom. This person was an advocate who had helped me with a complaint to the NHS about everything I had gone through. I managed to get a sit-down meeting with him to discuss my concerns with the maternity ward heads. They admitted that they had missed the chance for early intervention when I asked for something to help me sleep. I had also tried to get them to add a warning on the pain management leaflet for women in labour

, advising against using gas and air if you are prone to psychosis. But not enough people had come forward with the same problem. I thought probably not, as not many people make it out of their medications and realised it was the drug, not them. However, I've noticed in the last few years that many women are coming forward with birth-related trauma. I could not take the complaint any further legally, as no solicitor would take it on due to the time limits for medical negligence and misdiagnosis, or so I thought. So, I had to leave it at that and get on with my life.

I experienced the "flop" symptom, where your system simply cannot contain any more pressure, and you literally go physically limp—unable to do one more thing. I learned that the old motto, "Feel the fear and do it anyway," which I had always followed, does not work with PTSD. It only leads to more trauma. So, avoidance became my coping strategy, and that was not like me. I would be triggered by the slightest thing. For example, when we ordered a takeaway, I would be literally terrified about it arriving, and when it was delivered, I would panic about it being spilled on the floor. I could not relax until it was all on plates, and even then, I would be paralysed with fear. I remember when Rubey, about two years old, sat on my knee with a drawing she had done, and I was terrified of getting a paper cut.

If you are going through hell…keep going" (Winston Churchill)

I will not go into all of the issues I faced, as they're very personal and deep, but in the years after I went back onto medication and then off again, I seemed to go through every mental health disorder imaginable, all on my own. Then one would pass, and another would follow. In spirituality, this is referred to as *transmutation*.

One particular issue I experienced is known in psychiatry as "trapped behind the eyes." After awakening to the truth that I was a spirit having a human experience, not a human having a spiritual experience, I was initially appalled. Appalled at being human, given how awful humans can be to each other. Not to mention, they still go to war. I mean, how many millions have been killed in just the last couple of hundred years alone? As a relatively evolved human being, that's abhorrent. Knowing I was an infinite being inside a body felt very limiting, and I did indeed feel trapped in that body. Since the awareness mostly rested in my head, I felt trapped behind my eyes. It was claustrophobic, very disturbing, and frightening—something I could not explain to anyone. It was a haunting experience that lasted for months, present every minute of every day.

You're probably wondering how I got through this and found healing. Well, I knew it would eventually pass. I allowed myself to feel it and to be in it. It was truly one of the most profound experiences I've had, as it was at the very core of freeing one's conditioned human mind. I knew I was unlimited, but that darkness, isolation, and coldness were indeed heavy. However, with true alchemy in mind—*as above, so below*—how could I ever reach the light if I had not traversed the dark? And like a caterpillar instinctively knows to enter its cocoon of goo and destruction, I somehow knew that, eventually, I would be okay. Many times, I felt as if I had gained my butterfly wings over those years. The last two years have been easier, and now I truly feel as if I'm flying free.

They say life is not linear, but a spiral, and you return to points you thought you had healed, only to see them from a new and deeper perspective. I was also connected to many others experiencing similar things on Facebook—fellow lightworkers,indigos, crystals, and rainbow warriors—all transcending the darkest states of being to free themselves and heal mankind. Was it Gandhi or the Dalai Lama who said, "The only way to heal the world is through the transformation of the individual"? Thank God for Facebook. The people I met there—many of whom I still stay connected with, having never met in person—became my strength, motivation, determination, and inspiration. I became that for others too.

I became a full-time employee of the universe, spreading truth, conscious knowledge, and positivity. It was my lifeline. None of my family were going through the awakening experience, so I felt incredibly isolated.

At times, I really thought I'd gone completely insane, like someone who's taken too much LSD and cannot come back. I was stuck in so many insanity loops and went down so many rabbit holes that it felt hopeless at times. But I kept showing up—half a person on meds, a dysfunctional person off meds. I knew I had to keep going and that one day it would get better. During this time, I started having holistic treatments because I did not trust Western medicine at all. I trained in Reiki, levels one and two, and I found a wonderful spiritual healing centre called The World Healing Centre. It was a Christian-based charity that helped people with prayers from around the world. At first, I thought it was not for me, but on further enquiry, I realised they offered free meditation classes and other services more spiritually aligned with myself.

At one point, a GP who was also an energy healer— a complete paradox, I thought—came to offer affordable spiritual healing sessions. Being on benefits obviously restricted my budget, so I thought this was priceless. Both Joe and I went along. After my 15-minute session, which involved her attuning my energy, she "prescribed" me a book called *ET 101: The Cosmic Instruction Manual*, which she lent me. I read it with gusto, and it talked about star seeds and other spiritual concepts I had come across. This helped me enormously, as it reassured me that I had not gone completely insane after all and that I was from a different dimension—born as a human in 1971 but having lived past lives not on Earth.

However, being back on antidepressants and antipsychotic

meds caused another deep depression. This was not a dark night of the soul—I'd been through that in the early years of my awakening, a very dark and lonely place, but lifelong depression had been good training for that. No, this depression stemmed from the feeling that I had failed my mission. I thought that being authentic, my biggest goal, meant no meds. I knew that the tablets interfered with the pineal gland (your actual third eye—yes, it's an actual body part). Eventually, I came off them and began my journey back to self.

Do not get me wrong—medication serves a purpose. We all need a ledge to lean on at times. But I do not think people should be kept on them for life unless they are unable to cope with or understand the supernatural "symptoms," etc. Some people see demons, for example. I did, back in 2008 on the Avondale, but only a couple of times. I would not want to be seeing that all day, though. Others who have grown up with these experiences, with families and support who have insight, can live without the meds.

There's a famous saying: "The mystic swims and delights in the same waters the schizophrenic drowns in." It all depends on when it happens. If you're at a site of trauma, which is when this can occur (to anyone, by the way), and you have no insight, then yes, it feels overwhelming, confusing, and frightening. And because of our lack of understanding in the West, you feel like you are "mentally ill." Many future psychics, mystics, healers, and the like have been misunderstood, incarcerated, and medicated for what is, in fact, a spiritual experience. In the East, people are celebrated for these types of experiences, but here in the UK, we are often seen as an abomination. Even while I was on that psych ward, I knew, despite losing my insight, that there was much more to this than met the eye.

So yes, while on antidepressants, I was on Mirtazapine, a very old-school, heavy-duty tablet, and a high dose too. I knew it was too much, as when I spoke, I could feel my words slurring slightly, but by then, I had stopped caring. The antipsychotics caused such a challenge when walking. You could feel the chemical fog on the brain, making everything harder to do. With my back problem as well, it was a nightmare. I was in a mess at that point—I'd lost my fight, I'd had enough. Then one day, Joe and I just threw all the tablets out. This is notsomething I'd recommend to anyone on medication—always check with your GP first—but this was my course of action, and it turned out to be the best thing I've ever done.

This was about three or four years ago, and now I only ever take an antipsychotic if I've had enough and know I need to knock my brain out to sleep and reset. I was told recently by a psychiatrist consultant (I go to keep my records up to date for the DWP, etc.) that this was a very good and intelligent way of managing my "condition." This was the second time I'd met with him, and I even had the courage to tell him I was a star seed. I thought by now the services might have heard of it, but he said he had not. Still, I bravely continued. He had told me before the assessment that he was reading the Bhagavad Gita, so we connected on that level. My report stated that "Alison uses spiritual ideology to understand her symptoms." He said I was basically "warding off schizophrenia." I'll take that as a compliment.

During the last time I was on full-time meds, I felt like I had given up on life and myself. As I said, I felt I had failed my mission to become a healer. I'd wake up every day around 5am in a terrified state from anxiety and PTSD (possibly complex PTSD), dreading the day ahead, trying desperately to calm myself down. How I got the kids to school on the days I managed, I'll never know. I'd come home from school and go straight back to bed— not to sleep, but to hide away in my own personal cocoon of hell, dreading every noise, every thought, everything. I dreaded home time when I'd have to get up and support them. God bless them, whatever they asked of me, I could not do straight away because I was paralysed by fear, needing time to work up to it.

As soon as I stopped the psychiatric meds, I started to feel better. One day, I told Spirit (aka "God/the Universe"), "Okay, I'm ready, switch it back on." That was about three years ago. We moved house two years ago, and now we have our "forever home," which has helped me feel more secure.

It's now May 2025, and in two days, I'm heading down to Dorset to begin my Shamanic Practitioner Energy Healer training, Level One. For the first time in my life, I'll be using Passenger Assist on the train journey as a disabled person, and I'm not bothered by it. I've always been pro-human rights, disability rights, and mental health rights, and now I'm living that reality myself.

I learned about manifesting at the beginning of my awakening 11 years ago, and I was told then that I was a "magnificent manifester." Now, I've finally manifested my wildest dream: to be an energy healer and live as an authentic being. Even in the darkest moments, I secretly knew, somehow, that I would make it. I always had things about shamanism on my vision boards, and I've tried to follow the shaman's path as much as I could.

My disabilities now are mostly physical: my long-standing back problem, which they now call "arthritis," fatigue from my brain trauma, and just generally being out there in the "matrix," which causes fatigue and confusion in my logical mind. It's taxing, to say the least. Engaging with non-spiritual people can be very draining. For example, today, I had to abandon my planned activity after just 30 minutes of being "out there" because I was exhausted. I may learn slower than others, but I'll be giving it my all. I'm now known as neurodivergent (although not officially diagnosed), and my type is referred to as "acquired." Where I'll be training is dubbed "Hogwarts for adults." I know it's going to be transformative and amazing, even if it's challenging for me. I know that challenges are what build you.

The healing journey is notjust about healing mental conditions; it's also about letting go of limiting beliefs, conditioning, bad habits, and learning to understand yourself while putting boundaries in place. The main criteria are moving from fear to love. Learning to love myself has been a long journey, starting from simply learning to like myself with low self-esteem. Even though I had learned how to mask my anxiety, I appeared confident. My work colleagues could not even believe I had anxiety. My masking skills were excellent. Apparently, the higher your intelligence, the easier it is to mask your symptoms. I did not think I was that intelligent.

During this intense period, when I was still managing to go to work, I had a supervision meeting. At that time, I had complex PTSD, had gone fully psychic (what Western medics would have called psychosis), was self-actualising, spiritually awakening, and was shamanically "walking the worlds," which is basically like being on LSD. But she could not tell anything was different. I was what's known as a "top-rate functioned." This cost me a lot in the end. I should have gone off sick, but I was terrified of going on benefits and being put back on medication. Going to work and hiding all of this for three months caused severe trauma to my brain, which still affects me today. Plodding on like a Trojan horse, even though burnout, I kept going.

I do not regret any part of my journey. Recently, I was in a shop, stuck in analysis mode, trying to figure out what was going on. I was on the verge of feeling sorry for myself, but luckily, my spirit took over, and I thought, "Well, if we come here to heal and go back to love, I'm glad I am me. I always was hardcore. 'Hardcore till I die.'"

The anger I felt when I first came off meds after six years was intense. Before that, I considered myself fairly Buddhist, and with that wisdom, I knew how unhealthy anger is for the individual. But I was violently angry with the system for everything that had happened. It felt like learning to sit on a volcano, not wanting to release it in the wrong direction. I was angry that I had only been half a person for six years. I was fuming because, back then, before I understood the relevance of signs and symbols, I was looking for them to help me ground—I guess, before I knew about grounding. I went through a wobbly period and told my CPN about some signs I had seen, and from then on, they gauged how "ill" I was by whether or not I was looking for signs and symbols! On my final meeting with my CPN, they stated that this was a "natural part of my personality." Wow! For nearly six years, they guided me away from that, telling me it was illness. That was my innate spiritual wisdom, and I was condemned to more meds and higher doses when I did this.

Now, in 2025, I've made it—not just to receive synchronicities (which, by the way, represent how closely connected you are to Source energy), but now I'm swimming in it. Fully aligned with synchronicity. Oneness. It's my favourite thing about being human. I call it manna from heaven. Eighteen months after coming off the meds in 2014, I finally trusted myself enough to go for therapy, and I asked for CBT, having had it before. My thoughts were so muddled it took me that long to understand what had actually happened. The therapist was lovely, and after hearing my story, which he described as "dizzying" (I apologised for making him dizzy), he said, "Alison, you've every right to be angry with mental health services," which helped me a lot. He said, "What we are going to do is put a language to it," meaning all that had happened, and that's what we did. We did not really do much about the present; we were putting everything right in my mind. It took 16 sessions. I'd recommend CBT to anyone.

My whole life, I've worked with mental health issues—yes, I had time off sick, but I always went back to work. But what happened in 2008 when Katey was born, and then in 2014 when the trauma resurfaced, caused me to be disabled and unable to work. I had hidden disabilities before then, since the speed psychosis in 1993. But now, I'm hoping to work in small doses for myself, from home, as a shamanic healer. I know everything I went through was part of my training as a healer because you have to understand what it's all about personally before you can hold space for another to heal. Then your empathy and compassion reach deeper and are more authentic. In shamanism and Reiki, it's thought that whatever happens was supposed to happen because it's the thing that did happen. It's a very hard stance to take, but I've learned to embrace it.

The art of healing is to accept and love yourself where you are now, in each moment. Perfection is not required. Crying helps release a lot and is very healing, but it's important not to fall into a victim mentality, which is not helpful at all. "Why me? Poor me" does not help. Compassion and empathy—for oneself or any other, not sympathy—that's the key. Acceptance is also vital. Then, you have to face the shadow work, as it's known. Looking deep within yourself at all that is toxic and dark, knowing that we all have a shadow side. Accepting and loving yourself anyway. Basically, it's about making friends with your demons. It's not your fault what unconscious thoughts pop into your mind—just do not act on the darker ones. That's where one's conscious awareness and discernment come in.

All beings have the capacity to be either like a saint or like Hitler—everyone. When you've accepted this truth and done the work, you've balanced your light and your dark and are operating as a whole being. Learning to live, feel, and think from the heart—not the mind—and being conscious in decision-making, not allowing your life to be created from the unconscious. As Carl Jung said, "One does not become enlightened by imagining figures of light, but by making the dark conscious."

Once spiritually aware and awakened to the truth, you can see the problem with certain religions that place this darkness outside of oneself, like in Christianity. I am a lover, follower, and promoter of the teachings of Jesus. I actually found myself being baptised recently, but I know the darkness lies within me, not as a horned creature outside of myself. But this is awareness, and not everyone is there yet. Yes, there are darker elements in the unseen who can try to influence your behaviour. But to me, the devil and "God" are both within, and it's about tuning into the light or the dark. It's all about frequency.

On the healing journey, you must allow yourself to be vulnerable and let whatever comes up, no matter how horrid or hard, arise. This is where your strength lies—in allowing these things to come to light. This is where the real healing is needed. Find friends or healers who can hold space for you while you heal. Nurture your inner child by reparenting yourself, and the result is the complete transformation of your being. From the messy cocoon of the caterpillar (which we know is the destruction of the old form), into earning your wings as the beautiful butterfly you are. Transformation at its finest. Then, all your pain, suffering, and trauma are alchemised into joy, peace, and love for yourself and all beings, knowing that everyone is doing their best at their own level of consciousness.

Wisdom from this "cosmic shaman" ….

"Be kind where you can, but do not be a doormat. The more you raise your vibration, you should not come across what I call the assholes and dickheads, but remember, they need the most love. Sometimes the kindest act is to walk away. We are all one, so they are part of 'YOU.'

Know thyself, love thyself, be true to oneself, and love hard."

And as for the kids?

Well, what can I say but how blessed I feel to be the mother of two such wonderful girls. They are both strong, confident, well-rounded, and independent. Katey, now almost 17 (where did the time go?), has just left college after completing a year of a health and social care course and is now doing an apprenticeship at a children's day nursery. During her time at college, she got herself a part-time job at McDonald's. I was so impressed with her drive and confidence. I remember the first time I took her to a toddler club. I got her out of the pram, and away she toddled. For a moment, I wondered whether I should hide behind the pram when she looked back, but she did not look back, not once. Little Miss Confidence, even then. She's very well-rounded in all areas, living her best life with a lovely boyfriend, too. In high school, she was so driven and an independent learner who kept up with all her work, etc. I could not be prouder of her.

Rubey, now 12, excelled at primary school, with teachers always commenting and commending her for being an "always" child—always ready to help teachers and other pupils struggling with their work. A little lightworker for sure. Even now, she stamps down on any perceived unfairness among her peers, sticking up for those whose voices are quieter. In her last week of term at primary school, she got Star of the Week, and the teacher actually thanked Rubey for everything she'd done to help. Amazing. She's very emotionally robust, like Katey, but sensitive too. She's currently being home-schooled as she did not like her high school. She stopped going altogether, so I had no choice but to remove her. She's hoping to get into a different one in October, where her best friends go. She had a spell of not going to school just after COVID. She was off for three months then. It was a nightmare, as it was when I was poorly with the PTSD and all the other crazy stuff, and obviously, it pushed my stress and anxiety through the roof. I really struggled to cope with the authorities, always dreading a knock on the door. Now, I'm so over that. I do not buy into it anymore, the fear-based narrative. In Blackpool, if you've pulled a child out altogether, you cannot transfer them for two terms, so that's what we are doing.

She'll apply to her chosen school in October, and we'll work from there. If she cannot get a place, she may be permanently home-schooled. A friend of mine commented, "Aren't you worried that she's missing out on her education?" No. I went back to college and then onto uni at 32, so it's never too late to do those things. I was concerned she was missing out socially, but she's not. As soon as 3:30 pm comes, they're all chatting and arranging to meet up—she and her friends.

There was only one point in this journey of mine where I seriously thought I could not do it anymore, and I was on the verge of calling social services to put my girls in care.

Thank the good goddess that I did not, and I endured. But I do not blame or judge anyone in that predicament. It really is the hardest job in the world, and at that point, every day for me felt like swimming through treacle—bloody thick treacle. But my warrior spirit kept me going, and Joe, of course, was knee-deep in issues of his own. They say it takes a village to raise a child. At that time, in 2014, we had moved away from the only family we had, Joe's sister, so we barely got a break. No grandparents to take them at weekends, etc., so it was extra tough. But that's what we signed up for. Now, as they've got older, it's got easier for us both.

I'm not ashamed to say that the most challenging part of parenting for me was "nit management." Oh yes!!! If only I had a pound for every nit I've seen since having kids. I really could not cope with it and lived in denial, even with my own hair when I caught them too. So, we must have been known on the grapevine as one of those "nit families" for a few years. Nobody ever said anything, except the school and nursery. Mental health issues take prisoners!! And in that realm, I was one. The girls were not riddled with them, but they had them in continuous cycles, and it got worse when we lived at our last house, when I was at my worst. I was not looking after my hair, just putting it up in a ponytail without brushing it.

I was finding my own personal care challenging, so, of course, it got really knotty. Then I caught them, and I had no choice but to shave all my hair off. I felt like everyone was staring, laughing, etc., but I soon got used to it and spent a full year with a shaved head. It was the most liberating feeling, not caring about a hair on my head (or about catching bloody nits anymore).

Luckily, my nan was not alive at that time; she used to say,

"A woman's hair is her crowning glory," scolding me once for having a short style. She'd have had a heart attack seeing me with no hair at all. Talk about a mindfuck. Anyway, I'm glad to say this family has been nit-free for years. I'm also glad that, as they've aged, they've taken care of their own personal care.

I'm proud to say they've never gone without. In fact, they've been mighty spoiled, thanks to my husband, who is a survivor of very severe childhood abuse and neglect (I may write his story one day). Some abusers become abusers, but he's gone the other way, being a big old softy with our kids. He helped me to be a gentler, less strict parent.

I had already started working on generational trauma before I met him, but he softened me greatly as a parent. At one point, he could not bear for me to even tell them off, due to his own inherent trauma, so they were treated much more gently—emotionally and mentally—which I'm thoroughly glad of. They are free-range children, allowed to be who they are, but with boundaries and security in place, too. They have been loved unconditionally, and I am as proud of them as I am of myself.

Now, I write this on a train to Dorset, to begin official shamanic practitioner training. The timing is perfect, as my girls are older. I'm proud that they'll be able to see me doing something, rather than not really doing anything. And I feel I have a purpose again. They will see the "real" me now—unconditioned, deprogrammed, and ready to take on the next step of my soul mission. Eleven years it's taken me to get here, and I'm going to thoroughly enjoy it all. What a ride. It's been emotional, to say the least.

Thank you for reading this far. I hope you've been inspired by my story. Keep on keeping on, folks, but do not forget: even warriors must rest.

Wishing you happy trails and safe travels upon the earth plane.

End Note

This is not the end of my story — only the closing of this chapter. Healing is never finished; it is a lifelong unfolding, a spiral that takes us deeper each time.

If you are walking through your own shadows, please remember: you are not alone. The pain you carry does not define you; it refines you. Every breakdown can also be a breakthrough, and every scar can become a mark of strength.

I hope my story has shown you that no matter how heavy the darkness feels, there is always a way through. Always a reason to keep going. Always light, waiting to be found.

With love and solidarity,

Alison Hodson Robinson

Author's Note

I never set out to be a writer. I set out to survive. Putting my story into words became a way of making sense of the chaos, a way of giving voice to what so many of us are told to keep hidden.

This book took nine years to complete — a journey of determination, faith, and deep transformation.

This book is not a manual, nor is it a perfect testimony. It is simply the truth as I lived it: raw, imperfect, and human. If you take anything from these pages, let it be the knowledge that your story matters too. You are not broken. You are becoming.

Thank you for allowing me to share my journey with you. Thank you for seeing me, and in some way, I hope these words helped you to see yourself more clearly, too.

With gratitude,

Alison Hodson Robinson

Acknowledgement

I would like to thank my husband, Joe, one of the strongest and bravest souls I've ever met. He has taught me how to love unconditionally, in practice, not just theory. Without his constant love and support, it would have been a different story. He held space for me to grow and change while dealing with his own childhood traumas and mental health issues (and only calling me insane, I think, just twice).

Thank you,

X

To my two darling girls, Katey and Rubey. When every fibre of my being was screaming NO!!! It was my love for you and the love that you are that kept me going, showing up every day with a yes. I couldn't be prouder of who and how you are. Thank you for choosing me to be your mamma in this lifetime. It's been an honour, and I can't wait to see how your lives unfold now.

I love you all deeply, not forgetting, of course, Daisie and Alfie, the pugs xxx

To the healers, mentors, and kind souls, thank you for helping me see a new perspective, guiding me with your wisdom and unconditional support.

To my friends near and far, thank you for your patience, understanding, and for sticking by my side through the highs and lows. Your presence in my life has been an invaluable source of strength and comfort.

Thank you all for being part of my journey.

Published in Collaboration with Noble Legacy
Publishing
www.noblelegacypublishing.co.uk

www.ingramcontent.com/pod-product-compliance
Lightning Source LLC
Chambersburg PA
CBHW051259020426
42333CB00026B/3276